delete

VIKTOR MAYER-SCHÖNBERGER

delete

The Virtue of Forgetting
in the Digital Age

Princeton University Press

Princeton and Oxford

In the United Kingdom: Princeton University Press,
6 Oxford Street, Woodstock, Oxfordshire OX20 1TW

Library of Congress Cataloging-in-Publication Data

Mayer-Schönberger, Viktor.
Delete : the virtue of forgetting in the digital age / Viktor
Mayer-Schonberger.
p. cm.
Includes bibliographical references and index.
ISBN 978-0-691-13861-9 (hardback : alk. paper)
1. Memory.   2. Computer storage devices.
3. Internet—Social aspects.   4. Persistence.   I. Title.
BF371.M375 2009
153.1'25—dc22   2009014441

British Library Cataloging-in-Publication Data is
available

This book has been composed in Minion

Printed on acid-free paper. ∞

press.princeton.edu

Printed in the United States of America

3   5   7   9   10   8   6   4   2

To Birgit

Contents

CHAPTER VII
Conclusions 196

Acknowledgments

I t all began with a half page of notes titled "the right to be forgotten" in February of 2007. I quickly forgot about the notes, but remembered the idea. When journalist and friend Kenneth N. Cukier called to ask for new perspectives on ubiquitous computing and privacy, I pitched to him the importance of forgetting, and he included it in his report. My April 2007 working paper was quickly picked up by the media, somewhat to my surprise. My idea seemed to have hit a nerve. In the two years since my argument evolved, my idea has spread, and to my delight many others have advocated it or proposed something similar.

Among the circle of privacy experts and practitioners that provided me with valuable information, I especially would like to thank Jeffrey Friedberg and Paul Schwartz. Elena Saprykina helped me with Russian history. Marc Rotenberg, Nicklas Lundblad, and Philipp Müller offered succinct and valuable criticism. Edward Felten, Jean-François Blanchette, and Liam Bannon, who all have written eloquently about aspects of forgetting and memory, provided me with helpful pointers and offered most appreciated insights. My colleague at the I+I Policy Research Centre, Tracy Loh, read the entire manuscript and offered many valuable comments throughout. Ron Burt and Michael Curry deserve a special thank you; they took the time to read my argument and commented on it extensively with their inimitable mix of powerful encouragement and thought-provoking insights. I also would like to thank three anonymous reviewers for their very helpful suggestions. I surely have failed them for not fully incorporating in my revisions all of their many helpful suggestions.

I was fortunate to present (and hone!) my argument to diverse audiences around the world. Special thanks to Jean-François Blanchette and his colleagues at UCLA, Tom Bruce and his colleagues at Cornell, Thomas Hoeren and his staff at ITM in Münster, Doris Obereder and her colleagues at Ars Electronica, and Markus Beckedahl for re:public'08. Equally important, I benefited substantially from my many conversations with traditional and new media journalists around the world over the last two years; their questions helped me sharpen and develop my argument. In particular, Nate Anderson of *Ars Technica*, Lee Gomes of *The Wall Street Journal*, Clark Hoyt of *The New York Times*, and Kai Biermann of the German weekly *Die Zeit* all helped me see important aspects of my narrative that I had not been aware of before. I am encouraged by Alejandro Tortolini and Enrique Quagliano, and their campaign in Argentina to reinvent forgetfulness, and Bill Straus, who as a legislator aims for the same in Massachusetts.

If this book has an instigator, it is Tim Sullivan. Tim, a superb editor, was the first to get me thinking about turning my narrative into a book. Even after his departure from Princeton University Press, he continued to follow my progress. After Tim's departure, Chuck Myers guided this project with tremendous verve and thoughtfulness, and I thank him very much for taking on this book project midway and seeing it through.

It is befitting for a book about the virtues of forgetting that I now fail to remember much of the pains of writing it. I dedicate this book to Birgit Rabl, who has not only been its first reader (and critic), but who simply is the love of my life.

Singapore, January 2009

delete

CHAPTER I

Failing to Forget the "Drunken Pirate"

Stacy Snyder wanted to be a teacher. By spring of 2006, the 25-year-old single mother had completed her coursework and was looking forward to her future career. Then her dream died. Summoned by university officials, she was told she would not be a teacher, although she had earned all the credits, passed all the exams, completed her practical training—many with honors. She was denied her certificate, she was told, because her behavior was unbecoming of a teacher. Her behavior? An online photo showed her in costume wearing a pirate's hat and drinking from a plastic cup. Stacy Snyder had put this photo on her MySpace web page, and captioned it "drunken pirate," for her friends to see and perhaps chuckle over. The university administration, alerted by an overzealous teacher at the school where Stacy was interning, argued that the online photo was unprofessional since it might expose pupils to a photograph of a teacher drinking alcohol. Stacy considered taking the photo offline. But the damage was done. Her page had been catalogued by search engines, and her photo archived by web crawlers. The Internet remembered what Stacy wanted to have forgotten.

Stacy later unsuccessfully sued her university. She alleged that putting the photo online was not unprofessional behavior for a budding teacher. After all, the photo did not show the content of the plastic cup, and even if it did, Stacy, a single mother of two, was old enough to drink alcohol at a private party.[1] This case, however, is not about the validity (or stupidity) of the university's decision to deny Stacy her certificate. It is about something much more important. It is about the importance of forgetting.

Since the beginning of time, for us humans, forgetting has been the norm and remembering the exception. Because of digital technology and global networks, however, this balance has shifted. Today, with the help of widespread technology, forgetting has become the exception, and remembering the default. How and why this happened, what the potential consequences are for us individually and for our society, and what—if anything—we can do about it, is the focus of this book.

For some, Stacy Snyder's case may sound exceptional, but it is not. Dozens of cases of profound embarrassment, and even legal action, have occurred since then—from the attorney who cannot get the Internet to forget an article in a student newspaper more than a decade ago to a young British woman who lost her job because she mentioned on Facebook that her job was "boring."[2] By 2008, more than 110 million people had individual web pages on MySpace, just like Stacy Snyder. And MySpace wasn't the only game in town. Facebook, MySpace's direct competitor, had created 175 million pages online for individual users by early 2009.[3] Facebook and MySpace are primarily focused on the U.S. market (although this is changing), but the phenomenon is not a purely American one. Social networking site Orkut, owned by Google, has over 100 million users, mostly in Brazil and India. A good dozen other sites around the world account for at least another 200 million users. These numbers reflect a more general trend. The first years of the Internet surge, culminating in the dot-com bubble and its burst, were all about accessing information and interacting with others through the global network (call it Web 1.0, if you want). By 2001, users began realizing that the Internet wasn't just a network to *receive* information, but one where you could *produce* and *share* information with your peers (often termed Web 2.0). Young people especially have embraced these Web 2.0 capabilities. By late 2007, Pew Research, an American organization surveying trends, found that two out of three teens have "participated in one or more among a wide range of content-creating activities on the Internet," with more girls creating (and sharing) content than boys.[4] On an average day, Facebook receives 10 million web requests from users around the world *every second*.[5] As professors John Palfry and Urs Gasser have eloquently detailed, disclosing one's information—whether these are Facebook entries, personal diaries and commentaries (often in the form of blogs), photos, friendships, and relationships (like "links" or "friends"), content preferences and identification (including online photos or "tags"), one's geographic location (through "geo-tagging" or sites like Dopplr), or just short text updates ("twitters")—has become deeply embedded into youth culture around the world.[6] As these young people grow older, and more adults adopt similar traits, Stacy Snyder's case will become paradigmatic, not just for an entire generation, but for our society as a whole.

Web 2.0 has fueled this development, but conventional publishing—paired with the power of the Internet—has rendered surprisingly similar results. Take the case of Andrew Feldmar, a Canadian psychotherapist in his late sixties living in Vancouver.[7] In 2006, on his way to pick up a friend from Seattle-Tacoma International Airport, he tried to cross the U.S./Canadian border as he had done over a hundred times before. This time, however, a border guard queried an Internet search engine for Feldmar. Out popped an article Feldmar had written for an interdisciplinary journal in 2001, in which he mentioned he had taken LSD in the 1960s. Feldmar was held for four hours, fingerprinted, and after signing a statement that he had taken drugs almost four decades ago, was barred from further entry into the United States.

Andrew Feldmar, an accomplished professional with no criminal record, knows he violated the law when he took LSD in the 1960s, but he maintains he has not taken drugs since 1974, more than thirty years before the border guard stopped him. For Feldmar, it was a time in his life that was long past, an offense that he thought had long been forgotten by society as irrelevant to the person he had become. But because of digital technology, society's ability to forget has become suspended, replaced by perfect memory.[8]

Much of Stacy Snyder's pain, some say, is self-inflicted. She put her photo on her web page and added an ambiguous caption. Perhaps she did not realize that the whole world could find her web page, and that her photo might remain accessible through Internet archives long after she had taken it offline. As part of the Internet generation, though, maybe she could have been more judicious about what she disclosed on the Internet. This was different for Andrew Feldmar, however. Approaching seventy, he was no teenage Internet nerd, and likely never foresaw that his article in a relatively obscure journal would become so easily accessible on the worldwide Net. For him, falling victim to digital memory must have come as an utter, and shocking, surprise.

But even if Stacy and Andrew *had* known, should everyone who self-discloses information lose control over that information forever, and have no say about whether and when the Internet forgets this information? Do we want a future that is forever unforgiving because it is unforgetting? "Now a stupid adolescent mistake can take on major implications and go on their records for the rest of their lives," comments Catherine Davis, a PTA co-president.[9] If we had to worry that any information about us would be remembered for longer than we live, would we still express our views on matters of trivial gossip, share personal experiences, make various political comments, or would we self-censor? The chilling effect of perfect memory alters our behavior. Both Snyder and Feldmar said that in hindsight they would have acted differently. "Be careful what you post online," said Snyder, and Feldmar added perceptively "I should warn people that the electronic footprint you leave on the Net will be used against you. It cannot be erased."[10] But the demise of forgetting has consequences much wider and more troubling than a frontal onslaught on how humans have constructed and maintained their reputation over time. If all our past activities, transgressions or not, are always present, how can we disentangle ourselves from them in our thinking and decision-making? Might perfect remembering make us as unforgiving to ourselves as to others?

Still, Snyder and Feldmar voluntarily disclosed information about themselves. In that strict sense, they bear responsibility for the consequences of their disclosures. Often, however, we disclose without knowing.

Outside the German city of Eisenach lies MAD, a mega-disco with space for four thousand guests.[11] When customers enter MAD, they have to show their passport or government-issued ID card; particulars are entered into a database, together with a digital mug shot. Guests are issued a special charge card, which they must use to pay for drinks and food at MAD's restaurant and many bars. Every such transaction is added to a guest's permanent digital record. By the end of 2007, according to a TV report, MAD's database contained information on more than 13,000 individuals and millions of transactions. Sixty digital video cameras continuously capture every part of the disco and its surroundings; the footage is recorded and stored in over 8,000 GB of hard disk space. Real-time information about guests, their transactional behavior, and their consumption preferences are shown on large screens in a special control room resembling something from a James Bond movie. Management proudly explains how, through the Internet, local police have 24/7 online access to customer information stored on MAD's hard disks. Few if any of the disco's guests realize their every move is being recorded, preserved for years, and made available to third parties—creating a comprehensive information shadow of thousands of unsuspecting guests.[12]

For an even more pervasive example, take Internet search engines. Crawling web page by web page, Google, Yahoo!, Microsoft Search, Ask.com, and a number of others index the World Wide Web, making it accessible to all of us by simply typing a word or two into a search field. We know and assume that search engines know a great deal of the information that is available through web pages on the global Internet. Over the years, such easy-to-use yet powerful searches have successfully uncovered information treasures around the globe for billions of users. However, search engines remember much more than just what is posted on web pages.

In the spring of 2007, Google conceded that until then it had stored every single search query ever entered by one of its users, and every single search result a user subsequently clicked on to access it.[13] By keeping the massive amount of search terms—about 30 billion search queries reach Google every month—neatly organized, Google is able to link them to demographics. For example, Google can show search query trends, even years later. It can tell us how often "Iraq" was searched for in Indianapolis in the fall of 2006, or which terms the Atlanta middle class sought most in the 2007 Christmas season. More importantly, though, by cleverly combining login data, cookies, and IP addresses, Google is able to connect search queries to a particular individual across time—and with impressive precision.

The result is striking. Google knows for each one of us what we searched for and when, and what search results we found promising enough that we clicked on them. Google knows about the big changes in our lives—that you shopped for a house in 2000 after your wedding, had a health scare in 2003, and a new baby the year later. But Google also knows minute details about us. Details we have long forgotten, discarded from our mind as irrelevant, but which nevertheless shed light on our past: perhaps that we once searched for an employment attorney when we considered legal action against a former employer, researched a mental health issue, looked for a steamy novel, or booked ourselves into a secluded motel room to meet a date while still in another relationship. Each of these information bits we have put out of our mind, but chances are Google hasn't. Quite literally, Google knows more about us than we can remember ourselves.

Google has announced that it will no longer keep individualized records forever, but anonymize them after a period of nine months, thereby erasing some of its comprehensive memory.[14] Keeping individualized search records for many months still provides Google with a very valuable information treasure it can use as it sees fit. And once the end of the retention period has been reached, Google's pledge is only to erase the individual identifier of the search query, not the actual query, nor the contextual information it stores. So while Google will not be able to tell me what terms I searched for and what search results I clicked on five years ago, they may still be able to tell me what a relatively small demographic group—middle-aged men

in my income group, and owning a house in my neighborhood—searched for on the evening of April 10 five years ago.
Depending on group size, this could still reveal a lot about me
as an individual. And in contrast to Stacy Snyder and Andrew
Feldmar, few of us know that Google keeps such a precise record of our searches.

Google is not the only search engine that remembers.
Yahoo!, with about ten billion search queries every month, and
the second largest Internet search provider in the world,[15] is
said to keep similar individual records of search queries, as
does Microsoft.[16]

Search engines are a powerful example of organizations that
retain near perfect memory of how each one of us has used
them, and they are not shy to utilize this informational power.
But other organizations, too, collect and retain vast amounts of
information about us. Large international travel reservation
systems used by online travel web sites, like Expedia or Orbitz,
as well as by hundreds of thousands of traditional travel agents
around the world, are similarly remembering what we have
long forgotten. Each and every flight reservation made through
them is stored in their computers for many months, even if we
never actually booked the flight.[17] Their records can tell six
months after we planned our last vacation what destination
and flight options we pondered, or whom we wanted to come
along (although that person may never have made it, and may
never have known she was considered). They remember what
we have long forgotten.

Credit bureaus store extensive information about hundreds
of millions of U.S. citizens. The largest U.S. provider of marketing information offers up to 1,000 data points for each of the
215 million individuals in its database.[18] We also see the combination of formerly disparate data sources. Privacy expert
Daniel Solove describes a company that provides a consoli-

dated view of an individual with information from 20,000 different sources across the globe. It retains the information, he writes, even if individuals dispute its accuracy.[19] Doctors keep medical records, and are under economic and regulatory pressure to digitize and commit decades of highly personal information to digital memory. And it is not just the private sector that aims for perfect memory. Law enforcement agencies store biometric information about tens of millions of individuals even if they have never been charged with a crime, and most of these sensitive yet searchable records are never deleted.[20]

Neither is the United States alone in creating a digital memory that vastly exceeds the capacity of our collective human mind. In the United Kingdom alone, 4.2 million video cameras survey public places and record our movements.[21] So far, limits in storage capacity and face recognition capabilities have constrained accessibility, but new technology will soon be used to identify individuals in real time (as the BBC reports[22]—this referenced technology is rumored to have been pioneered by Las Vegas Casinos).

Instead of protecting citizens from overbearing surveillance and memory, policy makers are compelling private sector data collectors to perfect the digital memory of all of us, and keep it easily accessible for public agencies from the intelligence community to law enforcement.[23]

This may only be the beginning. Already a number of cell phones sport GPS receivers, making it possible to locate us and track our movements with precision. Numerous companies are marketing GPS tracking devices so that worried parents can follow the activities of their teenagers, or suspicious spouses the movements of their (unsuspecting) partners.[24] The first digital cameras with GPS chips have appeared, adding location information to each photo we shoot and every video we take, so that not only date and time but also the place of our mementos is etched into digital memory.[25] Soon the things around us may have tiny and affordable sensors attached that record their whereabouts, thus potentially providing third parties not only with a comprehensive digital memory of where we are but when and how we interact with the things around us.[26] Quite possibly, a more comprehensive trail of our actions will be collected than ever before, and retained in digital memory.

This is not necessarily all bad. In fact, in a number of ways an affordable and comprehensive memory is advantageous for us individually, and for society. Such memory helps us to note ideas and capture moments that will bring us joy and fulfillment when we look at them later. It counters the annoying side of human forgetfulness, reminding us of birthdays and wedding anniversaries as well as pledges and promises. Companies operate more efficiently when the knowledge of how its goods are being produced or sold is not just kept in the fleeting memories of its employees, but in a more durable form of information storage—from conventional notebooks to digital knowledge bases—that can be shared with present and future colleagues. Markets may become more economical when producers can use past preferences of its customers to predict future demand. Finally, our society benefits from remembering because it helps avoid making costly and dangerous mistakes twice. As many have argued, learning from history requires a societal capacity to remember.[27]

Yet, when we hear about Stacy Snyder and Andrew Feldmar we feel uneasy. When we realize how powerful and comprehensive Google's digital memory is, or the memory of credit bureaus, travel reservation systems, telecom operators, and law enforcement agencies, we are stunned. Equally important, our own collections of digital information on everything from PCs to digital video recorders, and from camera memory cards to digital music players have ballooned, offering us access to information our brain has discarded. What we sense is the demise of forgetting, and a fundamental shift to the default of remembering. And while remembering has its indisputable benefits, too much of it may lead to terrible consequences.

Privacy experts have been warning of some of these consequences for years. In fact, the birth of the modern privacy debate in the United States stems from opposition to comprehensive digital memory. Arthur Miller's famous 1971 book *The Assault on Privacy* was prompted by the federal government's plan to create a national data bank.[28] And the world's first data privacy act, in the German state of Hessia, was passed in direct response to similar plans by the German government.[29] Others have offered eloquent critiques of the growing use of surveillance technologies to track human activity, warning of a digital version of Jeremy Bentham's "panopticon," a prison in which guards could watch prisoners without prisoners knowing whether they were being watched. Bentham thought that such a prison architecture would force prisoners to behave—at minimal cost to society, thus a "new mode of obtaining power of mind over mind."[30] Sociologist Michel Foucault took Bentham's concept and argued that the panoptic mechanism has moved well beyond prisons and Bentham's idea of a physical structure and is now used more abstractly as a tool of exerting power in our society. In this, communication theorist Oscar Gandy connected the panopticon with the growing trend towards mass surveillance in our times.[31] The panopticon shapes present behavior: I act as if I am watched even if I am not.

Comprehensive digital memory represents an even more pernicious version of the digital panopticon. As much of what we say and do is stored and accessible through digital memory, our words and deeds may be judged not only by our present peers, but also by all our future ones. Fueled by cases like

Stacy's and Andrew's, fostered by our knowledge of the vast digital memories that Google and others have about us, we may thus become overly cautious about what we say—in other words, the future has a chilling effect on what we do in the present. Through digital memory, the panopticon surveys us not just in every corner but also across time.

There is no question, the erosion of individual privacy is a fundamental challenge we are facing in our times. But this book is not primarily about privacy.[32] Its focus is different—at the same time narrower and broader. Neither is it about the dangers of mass surveillance, the tracking of personal utterances and activities, or the rise of self-disclosure. This book is about the role of forgetting and remembering in our society, and how these roles are changing. It is about the potential effects this change may cause, and whether and what we can and should do about it.

Forgetting plays a central role in human decision-making. It lets us act in time, cognizant of, but not shackled by, past events. Through perfect memory we may lose a fundamental human capacity—to live and act firmly in the present. Jorge Luis Borges' short story *Funes, the Memorius* lays out the argument. Due to a riding accident, a young man, Funes, has lost his ability to forget. Through ferocious reading, he has amassed a huge memory of classic works in literature, but fails to see beyond the words. Once we have perfect memory, Borges suggests, we are no longer able to generalize and abstract, and so remain lost in the details of our past.[33] What Borges only hypothesized, we now know. Researchers have recently published the case of AJ, a 41-year-old woman in California, who does not have the biological gift of forgetting.[34] Since she was 11, she remembers practically every day—not in the sense of a day that passed, but in astonishing, agonizing detail. She remembers what exactly she had for breakfast three decades ago; she recalls who called her and when, and what happened in each episode of the television shows she watched—in the 1980s. She does not have to think hard. Remembering is easy for her—her memory is "uncontrollable, and automatic" like a movie "that never stops."[35] Instead of bestowing AJ with a superb facility, her memory repeatedly restricts her ability to decide, and to move on. It seems that those that have the capacity to store and recall unusual amounts of what they experience, feel and think, would like to be able to turn off their capacity to remember—at least temporarily. They feel shackled by their constantly present past, so much so that it constrains their daily lives, limits their decision-making ability, as well as their capacity to forge close ties with those who remember less. The effect may be even stronger when caused by more comprehensive and easily accessible external digital memory. Too perfect a recall, even when it is benignly intended to aid our decision-making, may prompt us to become caught up in our memories, unable to leave our past behind, and much like Borges' Funes, incapable of abstract thoughts. It is the surprising curse of remembering.

Forgetting is not just an individual behavior. We also forget as a society. Often such societal forgetting gives individuals who have failed a second chance. We let people try out new relationships, if their previous ones did not make them happy. In business, bankruptcies are forgotten as years pass. In some instances, even criminals have their convictions expunged from their record after sufficient time has passed. Through these and many similar mechanisms of societal forgetting, of erasing external memories, our society accepts that human beings evolve over time, that we have the capacity to learn from past experiences and adjust our behavior.

Despite the central importance of forgetting for humans, the monumental shift we are experiencing in the digital age, from a default of forgetting to one of remembering, so far this phenomenon has received limited attention. Back in 1998, J. D. Lasica wrote a remarkable piece in the online magazine *Salon*, titled "The Net Never Forgets," and concluded that "our pasts are becoming etched like a tattoo into our digital skins."[36] More recently, Liam Bannon, as well as Jean-François Blanchette and Deborah Johnson, have begun to uncover the dark side of the demise of forgetting.[37] In this book, I explore remembering and forgetting over human history and into the digital age, by examining what is at stake, and by evaluating and suggesting potential remedies.

This book cannot canvass all aspects of forgetting and its relationship to individuality, dignity, choice, and our ability to evolve over time; neither can it provide a silver bullet solution. But it makes what I believe is a simple yet powerful argument: the shift from forgetting to remembering is monumental, and if left unaddressed, it may cause grave consequences for us individually and for society as a whole. Such a future, however, is not inevitable. It is not technology that forces us to remember. Technology facilitates the demise of forgetting—but only if we humans so want. The truth is *we* are causing the demise of forgetting, and it is up to *us* to reverse that change.

The following chapter lays out the role forgetting has played during millennia of humankind; how externalizing memory has made it possible for us to remember even through generations and across time, but has never before unhinged the default of forgetting. Then I look at the technical developments—digitization, cheap storage, easy retrieval, and global access—that have altered the economics of remembering and facilitated the demise of forgetting. The fourth chapter maps out in greater detail the potential consequences of such a comprehensive digital memory, for individuals as well as society. Proposed responses are the focus of the fifth chapter. Because they fail to fully convince me, I'll add my own solution to the list. My suggestion is an expiration date for information to confront us with the finiteness of memory, and to prompt us to understand (and appreciate) that information also has a lifespan. Most importantly, though, my aim is to help us take steps to ensure we'll remember how to forget in the digital age.

CHAPTER II

The Role of Remembering and the Importance of Forgetting

We all know the feeling. We meet someone at a party whose name we can't recall. At the ATM, we try desperately to remember the PIN of a bankcard we haven't used in a while. We wander through a parking garage in search for our car, because we can't remember where exactly we left it. I know because I have been scolding myself in such situations for my feeble remembering skills. We may not like it, but forgetting is something very human. It is part of how our mind works. Or do you actually remember in detail what you talked about with your partner last week, had for dinner two days ago, or what exactly was said on television just this morning?

Human Memory

The human brain is superbly complex.[1] It consists of a hundred billion neurons—cells specialized in processing information. Each one of them has thousands of connections, synapses, with other neurons to transmit information. That makes for an estimated million billion such connections in a single person's brain. Contrary to popular belief that we only use a small fraction of our brain's power, the entire network of neurons and synapses is active in healthy human beings. But all the incredible processing and storage capacity of this vast network would be overwhelmed quickly if we committed to memory every sensual stimulus we receive.

Take the visual sense as an example. The average human eye captures a high resolution image—the equivalent of one taken by a 15-megapixel digital camera—many dozens of times every second.[2] With 50,000 seconds in the conscious hours of every day, even a very large storage system would quickly fill up. And if we add in humans' other five senses, the total amount of incoming information would be much higher still.[3]

To cope with the sea of stimuli, our brain uses multiple levels of processing and filtering before committing information to long-term memory. For example, from millions of individual impulses our brain constructs a picture, perhaps of something black and moving, and a split second later we "realize" there is a little black dog running towards us. That more abstract information—a black dog swiftly approaching us—is more usable than millions of individual bits of information contained in a series of snapshots of something black getting closer and closer. More importantly, it is also much more compact. As our nerve cells process the incoming information, from simple stimuli to pattern recognition, a tremendous amount of information is deliberately lost. It is the first layer of unconscious biological forgetting—and one we rarely realize.

Once an external stimulus makes it through that initial layer or after we have formed a thought, it is then usually stored in what's called short-term memory. In this state, we can easily retrieve it, but information in short-term memory fades very quickly—in a matter of seconds, eliminating most of the information. The psychologist Alan Baddely suggested that short-term memory actually consists of three distinct parts that are subordinate to a special control unit.[4] The first part acts as a short-term mental sketchpad for visual-spatial impressions. Researchers have shown that it can hold a few (perhaps on average between four and seven) "chunks" (digits, letters) of information. The second part functions as a short audio-loop, recording about two seconds of sound and speech. If not refreshed (for example, through constant repetition), that audio information is quickly lost. That's why we can hold onto phone numbers for a little while by saying them again and again. The third part is a short-term buffer of episodic memory, of things we have just experienced. Short-term memory is the information-processing bottleneck through which almost all information must pass before reaching long-term memory.[5] Once a piece of information is transformed into long-term storage, it is stored in what we call "human memory."

Actually, remembering is a two-step process. The first is successfully committing information to long-term storage. The second is recalling that information from memory.

Early in human history, our ancestors discovered that repeating certain tasks many times would eventually commit that task to memory. For example, as children of early humans first watched their parents hunt, then tried it themselves, time and again the process of successful hunting became etched in their mind, ready to be recalled when on the prowl. Gathering vegetables and fruits, cooking, sewing—these are all routines our ancestors learned by doing repeatedly, and which they recalled easily later. Scientists call this procedural memory. Such remembering is not a conscious act, but a by-product of humans engaging in certain routines. That's why it is part of implicit memory—memory that we acquire and recall without realizing it. After tying our shoelaces dozens of times as kids, we can't help but remember how to do it as adults. Riding a bike, brushing one's teeth, or doing somersaults are similar such routines.[6]

Declarative memory is of a different type. If recall from procedural memory is automatic—we do not have to remember how to ride a bike, we just ride it—declarative memory requires a conscious act of recall. Remembering one's first kiss, a severe illness or an exceptional holiday fall into this category. If we want to remember, we have to think about it, and actively "search" our mind to recall that experience or event in our past. Because these are specific episodes of our lives we have experienced, they are called episodic. It differs from abstract knowledge, which humans also have the capacity to store and recall: remembering the Pythagorean theorem is abstract memory, while recalling the context in which we heard about the Pythagorean theorem—for example, in high school—is episodic memory. Sometimes episodic and abstract knowledge can become conflated. Think, for example, of hearing Shylock's words during a performance of Shakespeare's *The Merchant of Venice*. What you remember you heard is in a sense both abstract and episodic, representing an abstract concept—words of a play—and a concrete situation that you have experienced.

Neuroscientists and psychologists are still debating what it means to "forget" information stored in long-term memory. Some think that information in long-term memory cannot be erased except through physiological damage. They suggest that when we forget, what we have lost is not the information itself, but the link to it. It is like a web page on the Internet that no other page links to. With no links pointing to it, the information cannot be found, not even through a stupendous search. For all practical purposes, it is forgotten. Unfortunately, the links to our long-term memory that are so essential to retrieval are not very durable. The majority of them are gone quickly, effectively depriving us of access to information in the sea of our long-term memory.[7]

Harvard professor Daniel Schacter is skeptical of such a mechanistic description of the human brain as a gigantic and precise, albeit imperfect, filing cabinet.[8] We must be careful, he reckons, that we are not caught up in metaphors of how digital computers store and retrieve information, and in the shadow of modern information processing conceptualize the human brain as a deterministic biological computer. In contrast to such a mechanistic conception, Schacter proposes a view of human long-term memory that is not unalterably etched in stone and from which we simply retrieve. Instead, Schacter suggests that our brain constantly reconfigures our memory—what we remember, based at least in part on our present preferences and needs. For Schacter, our memory is a living evolving construct.

Empirical research seems to support his ideas. Schacter has categorized research results on the malleability of human memory by categorizing them into what he, tongue-in-cheek, calls the seven sins of memory. The first is that forgetting over time is not following a simple decay function, as originally thought. Rather, forgetting depends on how often we recall a particular event, and how important it seems to us. Second and relatedly, we are prone to misattribute—to think we remember something that, in fact, hasn't happened. Often this is combined with what Schacter calls suggestibility—that our memory is susceptible to outside influences. Leading questions, familiar to everyone who has watched trial movies, are an obvious example. Biases form a related type of "sin"; they skew our recall of the past based on what we believe in the present. If, for example, after seeing a little black dog we are later asked for the color of the dog's collar, many will suggest a color with confidence, even if the dog in fact did not have a collar. Taken together, these effects reflect the constant (re)construction of our memory.

If Schacter is correct, isn't this a terrible fate we face: our past constantly altered by our own memory of it, fleeting and adaptive, and without any guarantee of accuracy? Is it this fundamental defect in human existence that has made us dream of and work on preserving memories since the beginning of human existence? Schacter believes the opposite. He argues that human (re)construction is not so much a deficiency as a benefit. Using generalizations, relying on conjecture, emphasizing the present, and respecting subsequent experiences, helps us to reason swiftly and economically, to abstract and generalize, and to act in time, rather than remain caught up in conflicting recollections.

Not just Borges but also AJ, the woman with amazing memory recall, would likely agree. Elizabeth Parker and her colleagues at the University of California at Irvine, who have studied AJ for years, believe she is a rare case of superior memory (hyperthymestic memory), with only a handful of other confirmed cases around the world.[9] Near perfect long-term memory without much effort sounds like a gift from heaven. No more misplaced keys and cars, forgotten birthdays and anniversaries, no more awkward moments of not recalling an old friend's name, and no watching a movie twice because you've forgotten you've already seen it. And yet for AJ "remembering everything is both maddening and lonely," writes Joshua Foer, who has talked extensively with her. Her exceptional memory has not made her any happier; neither has it made her phenomenally successful in her professional career. She leads a relatively normal life, but spends an unusual amount of time immersed in her past rather than enjoying the present.

Forgetting is not only central to our human experience, it is important for many other living beings, perhaps for life in general. In fact, the difficulty of remembering may be an implicit result of the second law of thermodynamics, one of the most fundamental rules of nature. It states that in our universe (as a thermodynamic system) randomness is bound to increase. There is nothing we can do about it. Of course, we can deliberately eliminate some of that randomness—for example, by putting gas molecules back into a sealed container. But doing so requires effort—energy in physicists' terms—which leads to more overall randomness (not inside the container but outside it) than we had when we started. Creating memory is producing some kind of order within our brain, which requires energy. Forgetting, on the other hand, can also be random, devoid of high energy-consuming ordering. Fundamentally, therefore, physics also tells us that remembering, unlike (random) forgetting, is always costly.[10]

For millennia, humans have tried to improve their capacity to remember, to increase the amount of information they can store and successfully recall. Despite the virtues of forgetting, it is easy to see why. Remembering helps us cope with our lives. Every day we are confronted with choices without knowing exactly what these choices will entail. Having to decide with incomplete information, our memory comes to the rescue. We use our past experiences—episodic memory—as well as general facts, ideas, and concepts about the world—abstract memory—in our decision-making, hoping that what we remembered from the past makes up for the lack of information about the present and the future. Aware of, and perhaps overly awed by how superior information recall can improve one's decisions and thus enhance one's chances of survival, our ancestors have long appreciated a human's ability to remember: those who could remember directions, or the movements of the sun, the moon, and the stars.

Two hurdles, however, constrained the value of human memory for tens of thousands of years. First, humans had difficulties storing and recalling abstract pieces of information. They had fewer problems recalling an event of their own past, an important kill they made, or the birth of their child, but remembering something as abstract as the Pythagorean theorem remained hard. Second, memory was contained in individuals. They had a limited ability to pass it on from one person to another. Knowledge and experiences, even though they could be enormously beneficial to others, could traverse both geographic distances and time only with difficulty. An expert in making stone knives could pass on her knowledge solely through the training of another human. Information traveled through the slow and cumbersome route of creating procedural memory, of individual sensing and experiencing obviously limiting its potential.

Language Aiding Memory

Language diminished that hurdle. Through language, humans can communicate with each other. Information that is passed on from one to the other can then be committed to memory without the recipient having to experience it: I can tell somebody that there is a water hole ten-minutes walk in a northerly direction, rather than having to grab my friend and drag him to it. Language also helps humans overcome their transience. Before the ability to communicate between people, having children (and thus passing on one's genes) was the only way for humans to preserve some of their existence for posterity. Language added a whole new strategy to prevail over mortality.

Evolutionary biologists estimate that language is a relatively recent phenomenon in the hundreds of thousands of years of human evolution. Only when our early ancestors began walking erect on two legs, with their heads slowly changing in shape, did brain volume increase, and the vocal tract alter its shape, giving these hominids the physiological foundation to control their sounds well enough to speak. But biological capability does not imply that they actually used it, and the lack of direct evidence—we don't have an eyewitness, or a recording, only circumstantial indications—leaves unclear when exactly our human ancestors began to speak. Archeologists and biologists debate whether and to what extent the Neanderthals, human ancestors living around 130,000 years ago and apt at using stone tools, had developed a language to communicate with each other. The current consensus is that, at best, it must have been a proto-language resembling song more than what we call speech. But in Africa, between 100,000 and 50,000 years ago, something happened. The sophistication and spread of tool usage swelled much quicker than ever before. It is difficult to believe that learning by doing—the time-consuming process of creating procedural memory—alone can account for this rapid innovation and adoption. The much more plausible explanation is the rise of language as a vastly more efficient tool to communicate (and thus to pass on information).

Language, as our ancestors quickly discovered, is superbly powerful. It lets people convey their experiences and their knowledge to others, thereby spreading them quickly across geography. Even more importantly, language enables humans to preserve memory by passing it from one generation to the next. This ensures that new generations can build on the knowledge of their forbearers. It also changes how time is perceived. Before language, previous generations, their experiences, ideas, and values were barely remembered, except implicitly through the formation of procedural memory. With language, previous generations become identifiable entities to which one can refer and which one can remember. Language enables humans to realize history, to understand a past beyond their own, and to contribute to it. With speech, narratives emerge that are passed on across generations. They may offer knowledge, or simply entertain, but out of these early stories emerged the grand narratives of humanity that offer meaning to life and human existence, and which convey a sense of time and history. All of the grand epics began as oral traditions, from the Sumerian *Gilgamesh* to the Nordic *Edda* to the Greek *Iliad* and *Odyssey*, often using rhyme and meter to facilitate remembering—and through language they came into being. And it is through *language* that humans grasp time.

The transfer of both types of declarative memory is facilitated through language. When humans communicate through language, experiences can be shared. Episodic memory is being created without the need to jointly engage in a particular process. Telling a friend about how I caught a bird is much faster than bringing someone along on the hunt to watch or do it for herself. That's a huge boon. But the impact of language was perhaps even more strongly felt for the transfer of general ideas, facts, and insights. If I want to preserve my experience of catching a bird, at least I can show somebody how I do it. But how would Pythagoras have passed on his insights without language? As language eased communications and aided in the creation and spread of abstract memory, it transformed the lives of our ancestors. It enabled them to pursue abstract thinking and develop general ideas about life and nature. And unlike thousands of generations before them, they now had an incentive to uncover these ideas, to understand the laws of nature, because their insights, the abstract memory that they had built over their lifetime could be preserved by communicating it to the next generation. The consequences were staggering. Language unlocked the potential of individual human memory. This enabled, as J. R. and William McNeill have argued, coordination among a much bigger group of humans than ever before, permitting larger communities to form and work together.[11] Language fostered the utilization of knowledge, and unleashed the powers of innovation and efficiency. In short, language was co-equal to fire in impacting human development.[12]

Despite the saying that talk is cheap, using language to pass on human memory across generations is not without its price. In fact, it is quite costly. It requires time and effort to communicate and to remember. Young and old have to get together for the old to narrate and the young to listen. Chroniclers have to be precise to convey the essence of the story, and recipients must concentrate to retain as much of it as possible. Quite likely, in order to increase accurate recall, these stories must be told numerous times for them to sink in, making this kind of remembering time-consuming and expensive. The effort needed for a narrative to be remembered acts as a potent filtering mechanism. The most trivial insights were probably not passed on this way; that process was reserved for what our ancestors assumed was central: knowledge that improved human survival—as well as grand epics that pondered fundamental issues of human existence and helped form a common bond among humans and across generations. Today, we have impressive technologies to help us communicate with each other, from the mobile phone to video chat. Yet, the technical gadgetry has not altered the fundamentals: human communication is still time consuming, and as a result, so is human remembering.

Direct vocal communication is one mechanism we humans have developed to enhance the power of our memory. But it has built-in constraints. It can only work when I have a counterpart that listens and understands, and thus is able to add to her memory what insights and experiences I recall and tell her. What if I have no counterpart to communicate with, or if those around me are not interested in listening? Despite having the tools to communicate, my memories are lost if I cannot share them. Sharing is key to keeping memories alive, and language is a prime mechanism of doing so. Unfortunately, sharing alone is not sufficient. Even if somebody is listening to what I remember, I might not be able to recall it with accuracy. Human remembering is pretty good, but as I explained earlier, it is far from perfect. Remembering is always a constructive endeavor. Through recall, experiences and ideas reemerge in our mind, influenced by our own individual development and the context of the life we live—as does parsing and storing what we have heard. It's like the game of "telephone" that children play, only worse. As children whisper a phrase from one to the next they interpret what they have heard before passing it on. The resulting outcome, the phrase uttered by the last child in the queue, often is a comical distortion from the original. In many ways, oral remembering across generations is like playing "telephone" except that we do not know the original story. In two ways, it is actually worse: what we pass on through inter-generational telling and remembering is not a simple "hello," but a complex set of information. In a way, this may make correct remembering more likely. An elaborate, gripping story offers rich context, which humans find easier to remember than a word or phrase disconnected from any meaning. Therefore, combining human memory and oral communication may preserve the central gist of a story, the epic adventure of life and death, of love and war. But it is unlikely that, through such a process, precise details will be maintained over time. This may be less important for an epic saga (for example, whether the dragon that Siegfried slew was green or brown), but is highly relevant when accuracy is important (for instance, how to farm crops, interpret the weather, navigate using the stars, or employ certain herbs to treat an illness). It led our ancestors to treasure humans with an ability for precise recall. A good memory was seen as a sign

of distinction; it helped greatly in finding work and joining societal elites, as Mary Carruthers has shown.[13] Plato[14] and Aristotle,[15] as well as other Greek philosophers, wrote extensively
on the value and nature of precise recall, and described useful
tools to improve one's memory. Human society's admiration
for superior human memory continued into the Middle Ages
and persists in modern times.

However, the fundamental quality of human memory remained unaltered: that storage and recall are constructive processes. Things become more difficult if we use language to pass
our memories on to others. The constructive processes of storage and recall then take place in two or more people rather
than one individual. The meaning of words and their connotations differ from one person to another—understandably—and
those that listen to a narrative without having experienced it
will have to quite literally construct the memory of it based on
how they understood the words they heard. Despite this structural imprecision, which kids grasp when playing "telephone,"
passing on narratives can bring about something like a shared
common memory amongst a group of people, but through
each act of human recall, listening, and storage its content is altered if only ever so slightly.

External Memory

If human remembering is the weak link, then perhaps memory needs to move from the brain to some external storage and
retrieval device. By drawing or writing, we capture an event, an
emotion, a thought. Looking at our own drawings or reading
our own words aids us in remembering, making it possible for
us to recall more, and do so more accurately. Used this way, external memory is an extension of our own human memory. Ex-

ternal memory can also be used to facilitate the construction of shared common memory. It happens, for example, when I write a letter and somebody else reads it: my words then become shared memory between the reader and me. When people share experiences by talking with each other, they too construct a shared memory. However, telling and listening, in this instance, happen at the same time (although not necessarily at the same location—if they use telecommunication devices). By contrast, with external memory, telling and listening are two distinct events separated in time. Telling happens when I write the letter, listening when the recipient reads it. Both are acts of (re)construction.

Painting

Painting is perhaps the oldest form of establishing external memory. It creates an image of a scene or an event, whether real or envisioned, and thus enables remembering. The oldest known paintings date back more than 30,000 years. Found in caves across the world, they often depict animals and their human hunters.[16] Relatively soon, paintings were used to chronicle events, and thus to preserve human experiences. At first, paintings were linked with the supernatural. Cave painters may have drawn animals wishing that this would make them appear. Pharaohs and their family hoped paintings would introduce them to the Gods after their deaths. Religious motives continued to play an important role in the paintings of the Greeks and Romans, and of course during the rise of Christianity and into the Enlightenment. But at the same time, paintings also recorded society's most important events: military successes (or defeats), societal growth and wealth, natural catastrophes like floods, draughts, fires, or widespread illness. High nobility was featured frequently and prominently, and interwoven in the painted narrative. As the grip of religion decreased and access to arts and artists rose, paintings transcended from preserving important moments of societies and its leaders to capturing impressions of a much broader set of individuals. It turned into a mechanism to create individual memories. Artistic self-expression, and strong religious and spiritual undercurrents were important motivations to paint, but so was the ability to capture and preserve a moment in time. Colorful and detailed Egyptian tomb paintings depicting scenes of the life of the deceased, vibrant mosaics of Herculaneum and frescos of Pompeii (conserved by the dry dust of a sudden volcanic eruption), and stunning bas-reliefs of the temple of Angkor Wat (now in Cambodia) narrating the history of an entire people are eminent evidence of art preserving human memory.

Such artistic remembering, too, came at a price. It was time-consuming and expensive. Highly qualified artists had to labor for long periods of time to create these impressive works of art. In ancient Mesopotamia, Egypt, India, China, Greece, and Rome painting was accessible only to a relatively small elite to chronicle some of their personal experiences. Through the spread of wealth during the Renaissance, particularly in the cities, successful merchant families in Europe could afford to pay a painter to capture a moment of their lives—but since painters spent many months, even years, completing a commissioned piece, paintings remained pricey. It took another two centuries for painted family portraits to become a common way for the middle class to create memory. Even then it was far from priceless, employed sparingly and with great care. Today, painting (like sculpturing) remains an expensive and time-consuming method to externalize human memory.

Preserving memory through painting has another, more serious, drawback. It is good at capturing a moment in time but not time itself, and thus is of limited use in remembering a narrative, an episode in an individual's or a society's life. One can easily imagine a painting of a decisive moment in battle, much less so how a painter would tell the unfolding of the battle itself. Of course, a sequence of paintings could reflect the important moments in the narrative, but it is a time-consuming approach and still leaves most of the story to the imagination of the viewer. Time is not the only difficult dimension to represent in a painting; abstract ideas or thoughts—like the Pythagorean Theorem or Newton's law of gravity—can be similarly tough to picture. Of course, one can imagine a nifty illustration of various triangles conveying the essence of Pythagoras' insight, and falling objects of various sizes communicating the core of Newton's principle, but such paintings would be open to many different interpretations, leading to perhaps intolerable ambiguity.

Script

Disappointed by the imprecision of human memory as well as the drawbacks inherent in painting, our ancestors looked for ways to externalize memory in a form that was not as easily susceptible to alteration and interpretation. In particular, those focused on the organization of production, trade, and administration desired to have a way to store and retrieve information with ease and precision. This was the birth of script, and ancient bureaucrats and accountants were its surprising midwives. In the fourth millennium BCE, humans in fertile Mesopotamia had formed larger groups, transcending small villages. This early society required organization beyond what was common to ensure crop growing, the exchange of goods, and societal supervision. To keep track of accounts and inventories, little dents were made in clay with a stylus. From these early pictographs, eventually writing evolved, as archeologist Denise Schmandt-Besserat has shown,[17] making the Sumerian cuneiform in the early third millennium BCE the first written language. Writing also emerged in Egypt roughly around the same time—using hieroglyphs—and then a few centuries later in China.

It was a breakthrough for remembering. Once writing was known and established, human experiences and knowledge could be stored outside the human mind, to be recalled at will and with accuracy. It enabled sophisticated irrigation and crop farming and furthered widespread trade. Writing facilitated the birth of the state as it eased the collection of taxes and the management of military and civilian power. Observations of nature and engineering insights could now be preserved, shared, and recalled with precision, and technological developments spread, making possible sophisticated constructions and fantastic buildings like the pyramids in Egypt, the Acropolis in Athens, or the Great Wall of China. But the advent of writing did not change the fact that remembering remained constructive, time-consuming, and costly. Early Sumerian pictograms were a laborious affair to produce and used sparingly. It took hundreds of years to reduce the elaborate pictogram to much more stylized (and thus less time-consuming) classical Sumerian cuneiform representing individual words. About 2000 different signs required a very sophisticated and highly trained scribe. These were hard to come by, keeping the price for remembering high. It took almost two more millennia for the number of signs to be trimmed and simplified to some 300 in regular use, thereby making writing more affordable.[18] The cuneiform were displaced by an even more flexible and efficient system of writing: the alphabet. By employing symbols that represent phonetic elements like vowels or consonants instead of complete words, a scribe no longer had to remember thousands or hundreds of different symbols, only dozens of letters. It drastically lessened the sophistication and training needed for a scribe, eventually increasing their supply and reducing the cost of writing, perhaps by as much as an order of magnitude.

Even with cumbersome cuneiform, scribes (and their masters) had used writing far beyond the narrow confines of accounting and bureaucratic recordkeeping that they were originally employed for. Literary works appeared, like epics, fables, and essays; some of them were fictitious, but many were also attempts to record actual events, experiences and emotions. These samples of episodic memory were now remembered by externalizing them, and conserved on clay tablets and papyri. Writing was even more useful to preserve abstract ideas and thoughts. Mathematical and scientific knowledge was captured, and by 2400 BCE tracts on politics and history followed, as well as the first laws.[19]

Writing also fashioned a new source of power: preserved knowledge. Leaders began to institutionalize collections of writings for their purposes. King Ashurbanipal of Assyria was perhaps the first leader formally trained as a scribe and was able to speak a number of languages. In his quest to create a repository of memory and knowledge, he ransacked clay tablets and papyri from the cities he conquered. With tens of thousands of texts on neatly stored clay tables, the library of Ashurbanipal must have been an awe-inspiring institution.[20] A few hundred years later, another project of creating a comprehensive collection of externalized memory attained world fame, set up by the ruling Ptolemy family in the seaport of Alexandria (now Egypt). At its peak, it was the largest library in the world, housing an estimated half million works. Unlike Ashurbanipal, the library of Alexandria contained mainly papyrus scrolls, which in comparison to clay tablets were lightweight and could be rolled up, saving space. The Ptolemys were single-minded and ruthless in their quest to add to their collection. They enticed intellectual elites from afar to come to Alexandria, research, write, and thus contribute to their library. Visitors to Alexandria were required to relinquish to the library all written

material they had in their possession. Important texts held
abroad were loaned and copied at significant cost. At one point,
Ptolemy III paid a huge collateral to the people of Athens to
loan some of their most important documents. He had meticulous and beautiful copies made, sent these "back" to Athens,
and kept the originals. The Athenians could keep the money.
But Ptolemy had reason for his callousness. He reckoned that
each copy made of a text would invariably introduce errors,
and thus diminish its value. This was why he preferred to acquire the oldest possible version of a text, hoping it would be as
close to the original as possible (or perhaps even *be* the original). In due course, this led to a boom in forged "originals."
Ptolemy's policies make explicit a process that had begun millennia earlier: the desire to have at a people's disposal a comprehensive, nearly perfect memory.

And yet, as much as script fundamentally changed our
human capacity to preserve information and enhance our recollection, it also exemplifies the inherent limitations of external
memory in general, and written memory in particular. This is
because, for us humans, the meanings of words change subtly
over time based on our evolving understanding of the world,
even if it is the same person writing and reading. If you have
ever tried reading an old diary entry of yours from many years
ago, you may have felt this strange mixture of familiarity and
foreignness, of sensing that you remember some, perhaps most,
but never all of the text's original meaning. As words aren't precise containers of information, each word and each sentence
necessitates human interpretation, requiring us to imbue them
with the meaning they have for us when we recall them. Literary theorists debate exactly how much our reading of a text
changes its content. But they do agree that reading (and other
recall from external memory), much like remembering, will always remain a (re)constructive endeavor at heart.[21] Thus, Ptol-

emy may have thought that by collecting originals he retained pristine control over meaning, but in fact he didn't. As much as the information in the texts he collected proved useful, it only reaches its full value when combined with what he could not control: reading and interpretation.

Ptolemy fell into a similar trap as a law school friend of mine, who had forced upon himself an intriguing system of improving his external memory. He had limited his personal library to exactly 200 books. Once he had read a new book, he would decide whether it was among the 200 best books he'd ever read. If so, he would add it to his collection, and discard the lesser one. Over time, he thought this process of constant filtering and deliberate forgetting would continuously improve his library's quality, so that he would retain in his external memory only the really important and valuable thoughts. What he failed to understand was that as his own views changed over time, so did the basis for how he evaluated and decided which books to keep, and which to throw away. Ever after decades of industrious work, his library will never be the collection of the best books he ever read, but an amassment of books representing different views and values, and stages in his life. What he, like Ptolemy, had overlooked is that there is no objective measure that stays constant over time through which we humans can judge the meaning and value of the words we read, or of the external memories we recall.

Scribes remained sought after professionals in ancient Greece and Rome. It required specialized training that was costly and time-consuming, and out of reach for the vast majority of people. But among the affluent, writing spread. For example, mosaics and paintings discovered in the Roman village of Pompeii depict a learned couple, with the man holding a roll and the woman a writing stylus.[22] Slowly, the scroll was replaced by the codex, a set of sheets between two wooden panels, bound together and resembling the modern book. While the nature of the scroll tended to preserve the sequential unfolding and the context of the narrative, with the codex, readers could at least in principle access a certain part of the text much easier than before.

Libraries continued to flourish. The Roman Forum of Emperor Trajan was not just a huge library, but also offered its users a place to read and work. Libraries cropped up in many smaller cities, satisfying their inhabitants' desire to have access to a comprehensive memory of humankind. Most importantly, libraries became accessible to the public. The impressive library of King Ashurbanipal was mainly for his own use, and the use of his most trusted servants. In contrast, Romans attached libraries to public bathhouses. Literate citizens could now bathe and read—with library holdings reflecting the demand for suspense and relaxation as well as the spread of knowledge.[23]

Books, however, remained very costly. They were one of a kind; each copy laboriously handcrafted by trained professionals. Even industrious scribes were only able to copy a few dozen books in their lifetime. For example, in the eleventh century CE a group of scribes at a monastery in England produced only sixty-six books in twenty-two years of continuous labor.[24] And around the same time, the Benedictine scribe Otloh is said to have copied a total of twenty-eight books in four decades of working life—a yield of less than a single book a year.[25] Of course, these numbers must not be taken literally. One cannot estimate the average productivity of a scribe using a handful of data points, especially since sources from that time are notoriously unreliable, and many handcrafted book copies were richly illustrated and expensively bound, taking extra time. But even if we take these factors into account, the output remained paltry, and the cost for producing books high. Schramm estimates that the production of one copy of a book cost a library in excess of what are 10,000 U.S. dollars today. Even the simplest and shortest book, for which a scribe would take perhaps three weeks of full-time work, would sell for the equivalent of about $700.[26] Such form of memory was an expensive tool, used with utmost care. By default, people continued to forget. This did not change for the next thousand years.

In the mid- to late first millennium CE, remembering became more expensive still—for most people. The Catholic Church began to usurp much of the script environment. Reading and writing was taught to monks in monasteries, who later the Church employed as scribes. These monasteries also functioned as libraries. Taken together, it permitted the Church to decide which books were to be copied and read, and by whom. In contrast to the relatively liberal (albeit socially stratified) Roman times, for a thousand years remembering became tightly controlled and organizationally centralized, although the spread of "silent" reading (rather than monastic reading aloud) made reading more efficient for those permitted to. The use of books as external memory was beyond the reach even of affluent people: they lacked access to the infrastructure to have books produced, as well as the training required to read (or write) them. Secular institutions struggled, too, and the grip of the Church eased only slowly. By the beginning of the fifteenth century CE, the library of Cambridge University had a total collection of 122 books, and labored a half-century to increase that number to 330.[27]

By about 1450 CE, a relatively simple invention combined with sociological factors facilitated important change: Gutenberg's printing press with movable type. It permitted the mass production of books, drastically reducing the time needed to create a single copy. In 1483, as historian Elizabeth Eisenstein writes, the Ripoli Press, a book publisher, printed Plato's *Dialogues*. In the time it would have taken a scribe to produce one exemplar, the press churned out an entire print run of 1,025 copies. And while Ripoli charged three times as much per original page compared with a scribe, it still brought down labor costs to a staggering 1/300th of the cost from pre-printing press times only a few decades prior.[28] The production revolution spread like a wildfire across Europe. By 1480, printing presses were operating in more than 110 towns in Europe, almost half of them in Italy.[29] Printing proliferated so swiftly because there was hardly anybody to stop it. Patents did not exist, and Gutenberg himself had gone bankrupt, leaving others in Europe to imitate his idea. More importantly, the Catholic Church did not grasp the consequences of Gutenberg's invention—at the beginning it even embraced it—and failed to stop the spread of printing that was directly undermining its control over books. As Eisenstein reminds us, in the fifty years from 1453 to 1503 about eight million books were printed, "more perhaps than all the scribes of Europe had produced" since the founding of Constantinople 1250 years earlier[30]—a staggering twenty-five fold output increase! Printers mass-produced entertaining works, as well as Greek and Roman classics, and comparatively fewer religious texts.[31] The control over memory was slipping from the Church's hands.

It was completely lost only a few decades later. In 1517, relatively unknown Martin Luther used the printing press to publicize his criticism of the Church, beginning a broad movement that shaped the entire continent, precipitated the Thirty Year War, and caused the establishment of Protestantism. By 1521, Luther had translated the Latin bible into the German vernacular. It was printed the next year, and very quickly became a best seller.[32] By 1574, one publisher of Luther's bible had printed over one hundred thousand copies.[33] For a precious few decades, the printing revolution advanced largely uncontrolled. States were just beginning to emancipate themselves from the

Church, seeing a potential benefit in reducing Church power. Most importantly, people wanted to know how to get to heaven without having to rely on expensive and ostensibly corrupt intermediaries. The vernacular bible they hoped offered direct admittance to God's thoughts, by then arguably humankind's most treasured memory. This hope drove people to learn how to read. Bibles were also read aloud in families and in small communities, multiplying its impact. By the end of the sixteenth century, Europe had been flooded with printed books and pamphlets promising access to God, furthering religious and political propaganda, chronicling scientific discoveries, reviving Greek and Roman classics, and providing diversion and amusement. An important shift had taken place: external memory had become mass-produced.

Yet, fundamentally remembering remained expensive. Of course, through the invention of the printing press labor costs had come down dramatically, and as the Catholic Church was losing its grip over the written word, demand for books increased substantially. But as printing moved from scribes fashioning individual copies to publishers printing hundreds or thousands of them, the cost of an individual book failed to decrease by much, because books were printed on paper, and the cost of this critical resource remained high—for centuries. In 1483, when Ripoli's Press printed Plato, they charged 90 florins for the printing. The paper cost another 120–160 florins, accounting for about two thirds of the total production price. Febvre and Martin, who have looked at the cost of printing on paper over time, concluded that cost hardly changed for hundreds of years. Well into the middle of the eighteenth century, for the printing of the famed *Encyclopedie*, 68 livres of the total 105 livres (65 percent) were spent on the cost of paper alone.[34] Even with the changes brought about by Gutenberg's printing press and the Reformation movement, for most people using books remained an elusive mechanism of enhancing their memory.

This fact wasn't dissimilar outside Europe, albeit for different reasons. In Islam, printing (instead of a scribe's copying) was seen as blasphemy, mocking the glory of God, and thus prohibited.[35] In China, printing presses had been known for centuries, although they employed woodblocks, not Gutenberg's flexible and efficient moveable type. Chinese remained a logographic language, more cumbersome to use than a phonographic one utilizing an alphabet; and the highly stratified Chinese society lacked the tensions that fermented the changes in Europe in the sixteenth century.[36] The Koreans, too, had developed a printing press using moveable type. Unlike Gutenberg's invention, however, it remained a tool of the court and the elites, who restricted the content mostly to Confucian works.[37]

Industrial pulp mills in the early nineteenth century finally lowered the price of paper, causing paper production to skyrocket. In Britain, it increased seven-fold between 1861 and 1900.[38] Together with steam presses and other advances of the industrial revolution, this enabled publishers to print more books than ever before—four times as many as in the eighteenth century by one estimate.[39] With the increase of the number of books, written external memory grew. Increasing numbers of books did get read—but during the first decades of the nineteenth century, only a small percentage of the population bought and read. Two reasons were responsible for the initially low rates of readership. The first was literacy. Only by 1840 had the literacy rate reached 68 percent in England and Wales. The situation was similar in the rest of Europe.[40] The second was cost—at least in some nations. Mass production and cheaper paper should have shattered high book prices. But as Simon Eliot has impressively detailed, at least in Britain, "the price of books was amazingly static" throughout the entire nineteenth century.[41] Books remained expensive. For the affluent London lawyer, buying a book was a relatively trivial expense. But for a laborer, a book purchase meant months of his disposable income. If one adds in the nontrivial cost of light necessary to read the acquired book at night (ordinary people had to work most of the daylight hours), books remained out of reach not just for laborers, but most office workers and others as well.[42]

Periodicals had been around since the early sixteenth century. By the seventeenth century, they had caught on with the growing affluent professional and merchant class. They also had the advantage that they could be shared easily among the readers— for example in the many coffee houses in Europe—creating the beginnings of a public sphere.[43] But literacy levels were too low and newspaper prices remained too high for it to become truly a mass phenomenon in Europe. That changed with the arrival of cheaper papers, including the so-called penny press, which cost about a sixth of a traditional newspaper. Literate lower middle class and working class people could finally afford to buy regularly printed information, and they did.[44]

In the United States, the situation had begun to change much earlier. In his magisterial work on the rise of the media, Princeton sociologist Paul Starr writes that by the early 1800s, newspapers were "more common in America than anywhere else," and "literacy was exceptionally high."[45] The leaders of the young nation saw the promotion of a robust and broad communicative space as a core goal to sustain the economic and societal development of the republic, and citizens were willing to dedicate time and resources to inform themselves of the matters of the day.

The other significant change was the introduction of cheap yellow-back books that catered to the low-end market—or at least those less affluent who were literate. Low-end did not necessarily mean cheap; while they were quite affordable in the U.S. (thanks to, among many other things, an advantageous tax regime), in Britain even yellow-back books were relatively pricey, costing a laborer as much as a week's disposable income. Only by the beginning of the twentieth century, when social reforms began to change the plight of the working class, leading to increased living standards and reduced work hours, did book and newspaper prices plummet and overall readership grow tremendously.

Shared Memory

This led to a new phenomenon in external memory. Through books, one could get a glimpse of the world. Newspapers similarly described the world in daily snapshots; read over time, they conveyed a sense of what had been, for each day. Affordable books and newspapers in the nineteenth century made possible a widely shared, if surely biased common memory of events unlike any that had existed before. To be sure, religion had provided a shared sense of direction, but it was founded largely on belief. Books have always played a role in constructing a shared common memory among their readers (and the writer of each), but for the most part they were not widespread enough to reach broad swaths of the population. Now cheap books and newspapers did both—they seemed to relay facts of actual events and they were widespread. What emerged from the mass reading of mass-produced print was widely shared societal memory. Through the act of reading, this shared memory grew, providing its readers with a sense of place—geographically as well as in time. Geographically, readers could position themselves in relation to the world and the location of world events, transcending locality, and offering—as Benedict Anderson so eloquently argued[46]—the chance to belong to a powerful, if imagined community, in which people felt connected to each other not because they were geographically close, but because they had socially constructed—imagined—a community of belonging. For Anderson, this links the rise of mass-produced print (what he terms "print capitalism") to the ascent of the empire and the nation state, both imagined communities.

Equally important, widely shared memory provides a temporal anchorage for the reader. This has profound consequences for remembering. As the daily paper turns old overnight, it consigns today's events to the past. For the daily reader, this past is not a hidden secret, inaccessible except to the initiated, but what she herself has read in days, weeks, and years past, and how she remembers it. Readers intuitively grasp that through the daily act of newspaper reading, the impression of shared memory is individually constructed one piece at a time. It is a combination of external memory—what is written in print— and the subjective connections and connotations readers establish to it—what is printed and how the content is understood and referenced by the individual readers. Through reading papers and books, people have been able to remember, for example, the attack on Pearl Harbor as a shared historical event, even though very few of them were present in Hawaii when it happened. They similarly may feel they "know" and have a share of the memory of JFK's assassination, the big East Coast blackout, the 2000 cliffhanger presidential election, or the terrorist attacks of 9/11. Mass media fosters the construction of a common shared memory beyond what people have witnessed together or a witness told a friend, and beyond the narrow confines of geographic proximity.

Thus, for the newspaper readers of the nineteenth and twentieth centuries, even distant events could transcend not just geography but time—and remain commonly remembered.

For such common memory to happen, what is necessary is not just a huge supply of affordable mass media, and an equally huge demand for it. That would not be sufficient, because with people reading vastly different works, memory would be shared only among the writer(s) and a small number of readers of a particular work. Only when the large majority of people read the same books and newspapers would many experience constructing a memory from the same source. This is not only true for newspapers, but for radio and television as well. When the nation still listened to a limited set of (networked) radio or television stations, what was said on the evening news became the foundation of our society's shared common memory. News anchor Walter Cronkite could say "and that's the way it was," because millions would remember it that way.

Views differ as to whether such a widely shared common memory was a good thing or not. Some think it enabled communication among people through a common understanding of the world, as they all read the same paper, and watched and listened to the same (or very similar) broadcasts. For others, such limited diversity of information upon which the people form their memories of events is prohibitively confining. But both sides agree that such a concentration of demand on a highly constrained variety of supply limits the amount of information that forms the basis of the construction of shared memory. If most people read only one newspaper or watch one television channel, fewer events can be communicated and thus committed to memory than otherwise. The net result is that in the traditional world of concentrated print and broadcast markets, external memory remained expensive—not so much in pecuniary terms for the recipients, but in available attention time. Apart from the relatively few events that are reported, for most events, shared remembering remained the exception, forgetting the default.

Of course, some external memory is not widely distributed in print or broadcast, but used as surrogate memory for individuals, helping them or a small number of others to remember: the diary that one writes, or the letter to a friend, a company's accounting records, or Grandma's recipes. Up till the end of the eighteenth century such external memory, too, remained expensive in most places, and was therefore used discriminately. Literacy was one reason; the high price of paper another. Industrial pulp mills brought the price of paper down, and thus made remembering cheaper. But it came with a crippling hidden fault. Pulp mill paper was not acid-free, and so disintegrated relatively quickly over time. Documents written on such paper had an embedded self-destruction mechanism, an automatic expiry date. This explains why so little cheap paper documents of that time exist today. Thus while more external memory was produced in the nineteenth century than in previous times, due to multiple constraints long-term affordable remembering remained elusive.

Photography, Records, and Film

The analog memory inventions of the nineteenth and twentieth century did relatively little to change this. My father grew up in Europe in the 1930s. When he turned ten, my grandfather, who was a circuit judge, gave him a Kodak Brownie camera. The first thing my grandfather taught my father was to be extremely judicious when taking a photo, as each snapshot would cost money. It should be reserved, he maintained, to capture the most impressive moments. In the next handful of years, my teenage father took perhaps only three dozen photos—of important family events, and the mountains he climbed. Some forty years later, I got my first camera, and I too was told that each photograph was expensive, and that I should take photos sparingly and with great care. I turned out to be much less judicious than my father was in his youth, but ten years of my teenage photos still fit into one thick photo album. Today's teenagers have no such constraint—the memory cards in their cameras hold thousands of photographs, and can easily be reused. But in my analog world of the 1970s, creating long-term memories had remained expensive.

As a quick look at the histories of external memory devices reveals, my experiences were the norm, not the exception. Portrait photography replaced most portrait painting by the middle of the nineteenth century; it was more affordable and accessible as photography studios proliferated, especially in urban areas with concentrated demand. With photography on the rise, painters from the impressionists onward aimed at capturing the sensation of the viewer, not the outward appearance of a person or scene. Not everyone appreciated the spread of captured visual memories. French writer Charles Baudelaire noted, "our squalid society has rushed, Narcissus to a man, to gloat at its trivial image on a scrap of metal." But the photographic technology used—the daguerreotype—was not cheap. These "durable mementos," as they were advertised in the 1850s, ran between 50¢ and $10 then, the equivalent of between $100 and $2,000 (in 2006 terms).[47] It would cost a worker's weekly salary in Britain.[48] Moreover, as no negative was created, daguerreotype photos were one of a kind and could not be reproduced. A few decades later, Fox Talbot's paper photography using negatives displaced daguerreotypes. It enabled Eastman Kodak by 1888 to offer a photo camera to people so that they could create their visual memories themselves, followed in 1901 by the immensely popular (and cheap) Kodak Brownie box camera. People finally had the technical means at their disposal to create external visual memories of great precision. Popular photography was still black and white though (and remained that way for decades), and by 1900 photographic plates sold for 4¢ a piece—around $5 in 2006 terms—which was surely reasonable for a special occasion, but not inexpensive. Taking ten shots at a social gathering and then developing the photos could cost the equivalent of almost $100 in today's terms, not counting the cost of the camera itself. By the 1940s, black and white pictures would cost a dollar a piece in today's money: affordable, but certainly not costless. The story is very similar for color photography.

Ordinary people began to have access to movie cameras in the 1930s, but they were very expensive.[48] Twenty years later, the equipment cost for both camera and projector had come down through mass production to the equivalent of about $200 each (in today's terms) for a beginner's version, but that of course excluded the most expensive part: film. Even into the 1970s when amateur movie making was perhaps at its peak, film remained expensive. An hour of film (without audio, of course) cost the equivalent of about $300 in many places in the U.S. At such a price-point, people thought twice before capturing something on celluloid, using the movie camera as they had the photo camera decades earlier: to capture special events and extraordinary moments.

Recording audio on magnetic tape became accessible in the 1950s, with the availability of magnetic tape recorders, but as with tools to capture visual memory, recording audio, too, was initially quite expensive. In the 1960s, standard tape formats—like eight-track and the compact cassette, as well as mass production—made audio recording by amateurs both widespread and affordable, although even in the 1970s at a couple of dollars a piece, blank audio media was never costless. It stayed that way until the end of the analog audio era in the late 1990s.

Analog video, combining pictures and sound, follows the now familiar pattern. At first excruciatingly expensive—in the early 1980s, cameras sold for about $5,000 in today's terms—equipment costs came down over time, reaching the consumer mass market by the mid-1990s. Televisions, the necessary viewing equipment, were widely available then in households. Tapes had become affordable, too. People began to tape hours and hours of events, from the special to the trivial.

But as equipment and media prices for capturing memories decreased and capturing volume surged, other formerly hidden costs came into view. With hundreds and hundreds of photographs and many hours of audiotapes and later videotapes, effective retrieval becomes a problem. If users want to be able to retrieve the external memories they have produced, they must spend time putting photos in books, or at least have them neatly sorted in envelopes and boxes. They have to keep exact records of what is stored on what tape, and update their records whenever they make any changes. This is not trivial. For example, many mass-market audiocassette players had notoriously imprecise counters built in. In a similar vein, as the capacity of videotapes increased from minutes to hours, so did the likelihood of forgetting what exactly was stored where. Because tapes are sequential media, locating a particular place on a particular tape not only required meticulous records, but also patience since rewinding and forwarding took time. There is no question that the amount of information people captured and committed to various types of external memory drastically increased over the last quarter century, but in the analog age, effective remembering was complex and time-consuming, and thus costly. Remembering still remained quite a bit harder than forgetting.

Since the early days of humankind, we have tried to remember, to preserve our knowledge, to hold on to our memories, and we have devised numerous devices and mechanisms to aid us. Yet through millennia, forgetting has remained just a bit easier and cheaper than remembering. How much we remembered and how much we forgot changed over time, with tools and devices emerging to aid our memory. But, fundamentally, we remembered what we somehow perceived as important enough to expend that extra bit of effort on, and forgot most of the rest. Until recently, the fact that remembering has always been at least a little bit harder than forgetting helped us humans avoid the fundamental question of whether we would like to remember everything forever if we could. Not anymore.

CHAPTER III

The Demise of Forgetting — and Its Drivers

Gordon Bell has been called "the Frank Lloyd Wright of computers."[1] He spearheaded the development of Digital Equipment's legendary PDP and VAX computer series, shaped the National Science Foundation's work on networking computers across the United States—what would become the Internet—and in the mid-1990s, right when he hit retirement age, he joined Microsoft Research. Bell is very much the smart elderly engineer, with a likeable smile, boundless energy, an avuncular kindness, and thoughtful insights. The only odd thing about him is the little black box the size of a cigarette pack that hangs around his neck. It is the most obvious outward sign that Gordon Bell, in his seventies, is again on a mission: a mission to remember all the bits of his life. His goal is nothing short of obliterating forgetting. "I believe" he said, "this is the quest for what a personal computer really is. [I]t is to capture one's entire life."[2]

For almost a decade, Bell has stored on his computer as much of the information he encountered as he could. Part of a long-term research project with his colleagues at Microsoft Research called MyLifeBits, he has scanned and stored on hard disk almost all of his paper notes and notebooks, including eight hundred pages of his personal health records. He keeps copies of all e-mails he sends or receives (more than 120,000 of them) and an image of every web page he visits. He audio-records and digitally stores many of the conversations he has with others; and the little black box he wears around his neck is actually a Microsoft-developed digital camera that takes a snapshot every 30 seconds or whenever someone approaches Bell, all day, every day; he reckons that he has more than 100,000 such photos on file.

The idea of a machine that acts as a perfect memory pros-thesis to humans is not new. In the late 1930s, British science fiction writer H. G. Wells wrote about a "world brain" through which "the whole human memory can be [. . .] made accessi-ble to every individual."[3] A few years later, Vannevar Bush, the well-connected science administrator during World War II, fashioned what arguably became the most influential descrip-tion of a perfect memory machine. In "As We May Think," an article that appeared in 1945 in *The Atlantic Monthly*, Bush de-scribed a machine he called the memex (for "memory ex-tender"), which "give[s] man access to and command of the in-herited knowledge of the ages."[4] Users would not only consult the memex, but also continuously add information to its mem-ory. Much like Well's world brain, for Bush the memex would "implement[s] the way in which man produces, stores and con-sults the records of the race."[5]

Vannevar Bush's memex never materialized. The technology wasn't there, and Bush became distracted with other ventures. But a little more than half a century later, Gordon Bell has achieved most of what Bush envisioned—and more. He has succeeded in creating a gigantic external memory of his life, which he can access at random in seconds, and with just a few keystrokes. So what has changed between Bush and Bell?

We have moved from the analog to the digital age. Modern technology has fundamentally altered what information can be remembered, how it is remembered, and at what cost. As economic constraints have disappeared, humans have begun to massively increase the amount of information they commit to their digital external memories. The size of such easily retrievable digital memory has grown dramatically over the last decade, with continuing high annual growth rates. A study in 2002 estimated that about 5 exabytes—an exabyte is a billion gigabytes or a million terabytes and equals a billion billion characters—of information are stored every year, at a staggering annual growth rate of about 30 percent. More than 90 percent of that gigantic pile of information is in digital form.[6] If that is a relatively accurate approximation, the amount of information generated annually should have reached 10 exabytes in 2005. And this is only the amount of information we *add* to the global digital memory every year. Quite obviously, remembering has become the norm, and forgetting the exception. Four main technological drivers have facilitated this shift: digitization, cheap storage, easy retrieval, and global reach.

Digitization

It has almost become cliché to call our time the digital age. The shift from analog to digital information has affected most if not all economic sectors and aspects of our lives. Only four decades ago, digitization was a relatively obscure topic. Today's mainstream culture is practically unthinkable without digitization. We listen to digitized music, take pictures with and record video on digital devices. Most of the files we create—from simple letters to complex designs—are stored in digital format, and forwarded to recipients using digital networks. The global phone network is based on digital code. Movies are going digital, and so are television and radio. Medical diagnostics—from magnetic resonance imaging to measuring our blood pressure or taking our temperature—render their results in digital format. Even our children's radio-controlled model planes, toy trains, and slot cars use digital technology. It is no surprise that MIT media lab founder Nicholas Negroponte titled his popular book *Being Digital*. And yet, despite its mainstream popularity, the digital paradigm and why it differs from the analog is as complex as it is central to understanding the meteoric rise of remembering.

In the analog world, stored information often is a relatively exact rendition of the original signal. To preserve sound, for example, it is translated into an electrical signal, which is then used to magnetize the surface of a tape. Unfortunately, when analog information (that is, information in the form of an analog signal) is later processed, stored, and transmitted, random variations—aptly called noise—are invariably added, eventually rendering the original information incomprehensible. Those of us who remember analog music cassettes know this phenomenon all too well: copying the copy of a copy of a really nice music tape yielded not another tape with great sound, but a mediocre one. At each copying process noise crept into the recording, reducing its fidelity. Copying analog videotapes led to similar problems, as did Xeroxing documents that themselves were the copies of a Xeroxed copy. It's as if in the analog world each generation of copies made to deliberately remember cannot escape a bit of forgetting—resulting in a slight random destruction of the content. Importantly, going back to the first copy (instead of copying the copy) does not eliminate the problem, since copying introduces noise not only in the copy, but (albeit to a lesser extent) in the original as well. It is what happens when one plays an analog audiotape too many times: the stored analog signal weakens and the resulting sound quality suffers. All these effects can be reduced with well-designed (and usually expensive) equipment. A high-end record player and amplifier playing a premium record through well-designed speakers produced great sound in analog days, but such analog memory came at a substantial cost—in terms of equipment as well as because of diminishing sound quality of the recording over time. And because random variances cannot be distinguished from the original signal, this "noise" can never be eliminated completely.

Digital information is different. Noise can be avoided, and thus quality does not diminish over time. It is easy to see why: As information is digitized, it is approximated as a discreet set of its parts. In the case of audio, for example, sound is digitized by measuring frequency and amplitude many thousands of times every second. Each of these measurements is a "sample," representing the sound at a particular (and very short) moment in time. Putting the samples together in the right sequence reproduces something that approximates the original sound. If the number of samples taken each second is high enough, for the human ear the reproduced sound is indistinguishable from the analog original. Similarly, an image can be digitized by using a grid of (say 1000 by 1000) little fields (colloquially called pixels), with each of these either black or white. This creates a black-and-white approximation of the original image. If there are many such fields and each one of them is small enough, the resulting image will be quite good. Photos in traditional black-and-white newspapers work somewhat that way— when one looks closely at newspaper photos, dots are visible.

This method of translating sensory information into discreet states, like a field that can be either black or white, may sound cumbersome at first, but it comes with a huge advantage. It drastically reduces the problem of "noise," of random alterations. Take the example of a digital image of 1000 by 1000 pixels that can either be black or white. When printing it on a laser printer, we translate it back into an analog form, and thus introduce noise. The printer may not work perfectly on all of the million dots, and some might not be as precisely black as others. If we scan the image again (and thus digitize it), we can tell our scanner that an information bit represented by a dot can either be white or black, but not ash white or light grey. Thus when our scanner encounters a less than perfectly printed grayish dot, it can self-correct the information of that dot back to black, and noise is eliminated. With digital information, most random variances—noise—can be filtered out, just as any signal (like "grey") close enough to a particular value (like "black") can be interpreted as that value.

Recognizing noise works best if there are as few such particular predefined values or discreet states as possible. Suppose digitization would encode a pixel as white, grey, or black depending on its darkness. Noise could change the information so that a white pixel becomes a grey or a black one, a grey one white or black, and a black one white or grey. These are six possible incorrect states caused by noise. Compare this to a system that has only two states: black and white. Noise might alter a white pixel into a black pixel, or a black pixel into a white one. These are only two incorrect states. Digitization does not tell us how many predefined states a particular system has. It could be one hundred, ten, or five, but it has to be at least two. Encoding information based on two discreet states only—black and white, on and off—is using what is called the binary system. Because it fashions the least number of discreet states, it arguably protects better against noise. This is one of the reasons why all common digitization today uses the binary code, and why information digitized using the binary system has become synonymous with the term digital information.[7] Remaining noise issues can be reduced further using sophisticated check-sums and similar methods. The result is that for practical purposes the digital information we are so familiar with corrects for noise. The consequences are profound: unlike in the analog world, a digital copy is an exact replica; every bit is the exact copy of the original. Hundreds of generations of copies of copies of the digital original later, the resulting copy is still as perfect as the original. Quality does not diminish, and copying carries no penalty. Neither does retrieving information—I can listen to the same digital music file a million times, and it will not wear out (my equipment may—and so may my ears, but not the file containing the information).

At first sight, this significant advantage of digitization comes with a stark weakness. After all, digitization creates "just" an approximation of the original. It is—at least in principle—inferior to the analog method and its precision. But the magnitude of this weakness depends on how good (or bad) the approximation is. If sound is sampled only a few times every second, the resulting digital recording is almost impossible to recognize for the human ear and is vastly inferior to its analog counterpart. If, on the other hand, sound is sampled tens of thousands of times every second, it provides a digital image that when listened to offers a superb audio experience. Similarly, if an image is being produced by translating a photo into a grid of 100 by 100 pixels that can only be black or white, a huge amount of information will be lost and the resulting digitized picture will be an extremely crude (and unsatisfying) approximation of the original. But a digital camera capturing an image using a grid of say 4000 by 4000 pixels, each of which represents one of hundreds of discreet colors rather than just black or white, is vastly better. It will produce a digital image that, at least to the untrained human eye, does not differ from the original. Using more information—sampling sound at a higher rate or having pictures taking with a sensor with more pixels—is key to solving the approximation hurdle. This is the reason why music CDs—sampling music at a rate of 44,100 times per second—offer better quality compared with analog audio tapes and analog audio records played on all but the most exacting (and expensive) equipment. The same is true for digital cameras using ten or more million pixels to digitize an image. Similarly, the latest generation of consumer digital video camcorders can now record about 2 million pixels per image captured in "high definition" for unprecedented quality, compared with a paltry 130,000 offered by conventional analog television.[8] Of course, the fidelity of such digitization depends not just on the number of samples, but also how well the audio and image sensors translate sound waves and light rays into digital information (this is the reason why, for digital cameras, more pixels do not necessarily translate into superior picture quality; it also depends on the quality of the digitization sensors used).

Because it lacks the noise problem, digital information is superior to analog information. Digital was bound to displace analog as soon as the technology was available to transform analog into digital information (and vice versa) fast enough and to store the amounts of digital information needed for sufficient approximation of the (analog) original. Once analog sound waves could be processed into millions of digital samples, stored on an affordable medium (like a music CD), and read by a device that could transfer the digital information back into analog sound waves (the CD player), the entire music industry shifted to digital. We have seen similar shifts in text processing, photography, and video.

But digitization enables much more than that. In the analog age, processing, storage, and retrieval varied among different types of information. This led to the development of specific equipment and a specific market ecosystem around them.

Consumers stored and retrieved sound using a tape recorder and blank audiocassettes. Prerecorded tapes were produced by music publishers and sold through special music stores. Consumers took pictures using special cameras and analog film, which were then developed by photo labs. People created documents by placing ink on paper using pens or typewriters—with paper, ink, pens, and typewriters sold through special "office" supplies shops. Consumer video was captured on analog magnetic tape in analog camcorders, and later shown on analog television sets—all bought in electronics stores. This elaborate type-specific handling of information worked, but it was obviously inefficient: We used many different information processing, storage, and retrieval devices in our homes and at work, and each one of them needed to be operated correctly and maintained properly to function. If we had a spare video-tape left, we could not use it easily to keep text on it, just as we could not easily use paper to store music.

In the digital world, all information is stored as binary signals, and all equipment is—at least in principle—able to handle such digital information. As long as information can be digitized, it can be stored on a digital storage device, irrespective of whether the information represents sound, video, text, or any other type. People can put Beethoven and their wedding movie, plus their latest business plan, on the same hard disk without running the risk of mixing things up or otherwise harming their information. Standardization leads to efficiencies through scale economies, offering huge market opportunities for producers of digital storage devices since they can be used to store *all* types of digital information. Produced in very large numbers, unit prices for these devices have been coming down dramatically. Standardization also fuels the demand for a general-purpose information processing device that can edit text, images, sound, and video as long as the necessary input and output gadgets (microphone and speakers, camera and screen, keyboard and printer) are attached. The personal computer owes its meteoric rise and current dominant position in information processing at least partially to this general-purpose demand driven by digitization.

The advantages of standardization extend to information sharing and distribution through networks small and big. Analog information is shared and distributed in separate infrastructures depending on the information type. Newspapers are sent by truck to local sellers, movies are shipped to cinemas; analog radio is using a system of transmitters. In contrast, digitized information can travel through the same digital network irrespective of the content. Sharing one rather than using separate distribution networks is obviously significantly more efficient.

Standardizing on digital information has another advantage. It is more "future-proof" than analog counterparts. As long as a signal can be digitized, it can be processed using standard digital information devices like personal computers, stored in off-the-shelf storage products like hard disks, and transmitted across the world using the Internet. The evolution of the Internet itself is an excellent case in point. Initially, the Internet was used to share a computer's information processing power among multiple (distant) users. Later, file transfer and e-mail were added as new services using the *same* network. And when Tim Berners-Lee invented the WorldWideWeb, it rested on existing Internet infrastructure, just like later streaming audio and video as well as Internet telephony (called voice-over-IP). Of course, over time the Internet's plumbing has been updated and revised, but its basic building principles have remained stable. The "future-proof" foundation of the Internet as a global digital network means that it has not had to be abandoned, replaced, or even fundamentally altered to make possible instant messaging, online gaming, even interacting in complex virtual worlds like SecondLife.

Eliminating noise while preserving fidelity, combined with a drastically increased efficiency through standardization, scale economies, and better resource allocation, digitization has made possible fundamental improvements to information processing, storage, and retrieval. But its impact goes beyond the obviousness of economics. By eliminating noise, the incremental forgetting inherent in analog technology, the notion of originals and copies is rapidly becoming an outdated concept. All digital copies are indistinguishable from the original. This has the advantage of giving everyone who possesses a "copy" perfect access to all of the information and value of the "original." The perfection of digital copies has greatly eased the distribution of high-quality information. Thanks to it, today we can enjoy high-fidelity music and high-definition video. Our affordable cameras produce photos at a resolution practically impossible for amateurs in analog times. And we can share them with millions of others without them or us having to suffer a reduction of quality resulting from wide distribution and repeated copying.

Not everybody is happy about the lossless, cheap, and easy copying of digital information. Owners of content fear that people copy without paying. In the analog age, noise—slow but inescapable forgetting—acted as a barrier against mass unauthorized copying. Just think of a copy of a bootleg analog music tape sounding mediocre rather than of high quality due to analog degradation; it may have prompted consumers to buy an authorized copy, made straight from a master tape (or more likely one generation removed from it). If, on the other hand, an unauthorized copy is as good as the original, getting consumers to pay to receive the legal version is harder; it may require offering additional value (something publishers have been experimenting through the iTunes Music Store and similar ventures) or calling the cops.

Irrespective of these rights issues, however, the easy access to and sharing of digital information across the nation and around the world has vastly increased what I have termed shared societal memory. Not only has societal memory increased in size, it has also become globally accessible. A few years ago I was strolling through the only shopping mall in the capital of the tiny but oil-rich Islamic sultanate of Brunei on the island of Borneo in Southeast Asia. I noticed a store advertising obviously bootlegged DVDs of the famous U.S. cable television series *Sex in the City*. At first I was taken aback that such explicit content would be so openly sold in a traditional Islamic society; but if we consider existing global information flows through satellite television, bootlegged DVDs and CDs, and the Internet, it is easy to understand that the people in Brunei wanted to follow Carrie Bradshaw's journey through the Manhattan dating scene as much as those in Cincinnati or Rome. Due to the global reach of mass media, shared memory has long gone international, if not global, and digitization has made possible a larger and more globally shared memory than has been possible in analog times. At the same time, though, it may oddly also have furthered the fragmentation of this shared memory since people are empowered to select how much and what part of such societal memory they want to expose themselves to.

That a digital copy is as good as the original has also changed how people, especially those that grew up in the digital age, perceive information. If in analog times it was cool to *own* lots of books or music records or movies, in the digital age it is cool to *build on them*—to take the artifacts of our information culture and combine them into something new, something original. As Apple's Steve Jobs famously described it for music: rip, mix, burn. Perhaps even add one's own content. The emphasis, though, is on mixing and recombining, on creating a *bricolage* as the former head of famed Xerox PARC John Seely Brown has suggested, in which the value is derived from the (re)combination of its parts, not necessarily from the parts themselves.[9] Siva Vaidhyanathan has offered the example of "Goblin edits," when creative Russian artists take western blockbuster movies and re-dub them into Russian, giving these movies substantially altered narratives.[10] As digital culture emphasizes recombining and sharing over owning, people are utilizing the power that digitization offers them.

In short, digitization is the enabler of a new generation of information processing, storage, retrieval, and sharing that is vastly superior to its analog counterparts.

Cheap Storage

In the early 1940s, when digital processing began in earnest, digital storage was excruciatingly expensive. The first successful commercial computer, the UNIVAC, had 12,000 characters (bytes) of main memory, and a magnetic tape drive for mass storage. A tape could hold up to one megabyte. UNIVACs then sold for a million dollars, the equivalent of about $7.5 million in current U.S. terms. Magnetic tapes were a useful innovation, but in addition to high cost they were also slow in retrieving data: if a particular piece of information was stored at the end of a 1,200-foot tape, the entire tape had to be run through to retrieve it. Engineers looked for storage technologies that offered much shorter access times. Magnetic drums were a first step, but expensive and of limited storage capacity. In 1957, IBM introduced the 305, a computer with magnetic disks as storage devices that offered up to 5 megabytes of space, and which was valued at around $1 million (in 2006 terms). The cost of the storage unit alone ran to about $70,000 per megabyte in the 1950s; by 1980 that price had come down to below $500 (all in 2006 U.S. dollars), less than one percent of what it had been just two-and-a-half decades earlier.[11] Twenty years later, in 2000, storage cost had plummeted to about 1¢, 1/50,000th of what it was in 1980. And in 2008, the cost of storage for one megabyte of information had been reduced to one hundredth of a cent. For fifty years the cost of storage had roughly been cut in half every two years, while storage density increased 50-million fold from 2,000 information bits per square inch in 1956 to 100 billion bits in 2005.[12]

Hard disk cost is not proportional to storage size. Because hard disks are essentially magnetic platters driven by an electrical motor and spinning at a couple of thousand revolutions a minute, some portion of the overall cost is always spent on these necessary mechanical parts. Chip-based storage is not saddled with such a disadvantage. This is why we have seen a steady rise over the last decade in the use of non-volatile silicon-based, so-called solid-state, memory. Digital cameras, cell phones and music players all use "flash memory." Initially relatively expensive, cost per megabyte of storage for memory cards has come down just as dramatically as for their hard disk–based siblings, reaching about a third of a cent per megabyte of storage in 2008—a price/cost ratio hard disk storage achieved in 2001, but with the advantage that solid-state memory does not require mechanical parts.

From the beginning of silicon-based integrated circuits, engineers have been able to shrink the size of individual components on these circuits, cramming more of them onto the same space. In 1965, an engineer named Gordon Moore wrote, "[C]omplexity of integrated circuits has approximately doubled every year since their introduction. Cost per function has decreased several thousand-fold [...] The rate of increase of complexity can be expected to change slope in the next few years. [...] The new slope might approximate a doubling every two years."[13] What was intended as a ballpark observation has held true for more than four decades, and Moore's "law" has become the shorthand term for the doubling in circuit complexity every eighteen months that we have witnessed since. Gordon Moore did well, too; he co-founded chip-making giant Intel. Because solid-state memory is nothing but sophisticated integrated circuitry, Moore's law continues to apply to it as well. The only fundamental disadvantage of current technology is that flash memory slowly wears out; it becomes unreliable when information has been erased and written-over about 100,000 times—not a very likely event (and thus not much of a disadvantage) for a longer-term storage medium.[14]

For some decades now, optical systems have played an important supplementary role in digital storage. On the consumer level, this has led to the widespread use of CDs (introduced in 1982, with a capacity of 650 million bytes), DVDs (1995; storing seven to thirteen times the amount of a CD), and Blu-ray Disks (2006; about forty to eighty times larger in storage than a CD). The comparatively slow pace of storage capacity growth in optical systems is not necessarily a sign of technical limitations, but of user preferences. Optical storage development is based on removable media (optical disks). When the underlying technology switches from one system to another, recorded removable media of the older technology may no longer be playable or not in the quality expected by users on the newer devices—a familiar situation, for example, for those who still own a large collection of movies on old analog VHS cassettes. Since consumers have invested in recorded media, they are reluctant to switch. These perceived switching costs constrain how often a new generation of such storage systems can achieve market success. To reduce switching costs, equipment manufacturers deliberately designed DVD and Blue Ray drives so they could also read the older formats, thus ensuring at least some backward compatibility, but these solutions are workarounds. The situation is vastly different for hard disks. Because there is no removable medium, when the technology of hard disks changes, users do not care. For them a hard disk is a black box. As long as it stores and remembers, the underlying technical plumbing is irrelevant. Thus, new technological advancements in hard disk storage can be brought to market much quicker and without fear of switching costs.

Plummeting storage prices have been welcomed by users. When they reached levels that individuals could afford for their personal use, it opened up long-term digital storage to the masses. It is also unlikely that consumers will be running out of storage any time soon—by the time one has filled up her hard disk, a newer one is available with double or triple the amount of storage capacity.[15] Gordon Bell reckons that people no longer will be able to be short of hard disk space. Bell may be surprised to see how easy even a couple of hundred gigabytes can be filled with high-definition video, but he is right in the sense that the increase in storage capacity continues to match human appetite for additional storage space.[16]

At some point, digital storage for a piece of information becomes cheaper than its analog counterpart. A page of text, single-spaced, contains about 2,000 bytes of information. The cost of a laser-printed page has been fairly stable at around 10¢, so that producing an analog rendition of a megabyte worth of text costs about $50. By 1987, digital storage on magnetic hard disks had dropped to $40 per megabyte, below the cost of the analog equivalent. Since then digital storage has not only been more convenient, but literally cheaper than printing and keeping conventional hardcopies. Or take images: conventional

photos cost about 30¢ a print. By 1997, digital storage had become so cheap that storing an image in digital format was more
affordable than paying for conventional film prints (assuming a
3 megabyte image file). By 2000, it was cheaper to store a music
file in digital format on a hard disk than on blank analog music
cassettes, making conventional cassette tape recorders truly
uneconomical. And by 2006, it had become cheaper to store
consumer videos on hard disks than buying blank analog cam-
corder videotape. Taken together—and even accounting for
backup copies—digital storage for consumer usage is now significantly cheaper than the analog counterparts to conserve the
memories of our lives and thoughts.

This may sound staggering, but there is an even more important dimension of cheap storage. As hard disk manufacturers quickly realized, given a choice, consumers prefer higher-
capacity hard disks at a constant price to same size storage
devices at ever-lower costs—at least once storage reached a
price level that consumers were comfortable with. Rather than
saving money, users want to utilize digital storage to preserve
more and more information. As a result, the cost of hard disks
has roughly been stable, but storage capacity of the hard disks
we use has skyrocketed. This is why our personal computers
offer hard disk space in terabytes—a million megabytes—but
cost about the same as twenty years ago; our digital music players contain many hundreds of hours of music; and the flash
memory cards in our digital cameras can hold thousands of
high-resolution images.

Two sets of driving factors have made this fantastic increase
in cheap storage possible.[17] The first set operates on the development and production side. Storage devices, whether hard
disks or silicone chips, are mass-produced in large quantities yet
must conform to exacting production standards. Initially, production is error prone, resulting in low yield. As manufacturers

fine-tune the production process, yields are pushed up, and scale economies of production bring down cost. This continues until further refinement of the production process becomes more expensive than the gains in yield they produce. Manufacturers also aim at product innovation, hoping to switch to a new product whenever yield improvements have bottomed out. Such new products offer significant improvements in storage capacity, but initially, as production ramps up, manufacturing yields are low. In parallel, market demand for storage swells, causing a market pull for manufacturers to drive up storage capacity and lower cost. Moreover, demand increases as the lowered cost of storage makes information storage and retrieval devices affordable to new groups of people—when a personal computer is available for a couple of hundred dollars, many more people can afford one. At the same time, available storage space and further digitization will make it possible for additional types of information (text, images, audio, video, spatial data) to transition to digital devices, again stimulating demand—the rise of digital cameras, for example, has fueled demand as digital camera users store photos on general-purpose hard disks.

Let's recap: Digital storage has gotten so cheap that storing information—even full-screen videos—on digital memory is cheaper than the analog information storage counterparts of paper, film, and tape. It makes it possible to preserve the tremendous amount of information we encounter and generate, much like Gordon Bell, who is far along in capturing his entire life on digital media—the digital equivalent of decades of thoughts and notes in his notebooks and papers, a hundred thousand photographs, hundreds of hours of audio, and thousands of images capturing web sites he visited. He reckons that he has amassed about 100 gigabytes of information, not even filling a third of a typical laptop computer's hard disk (he may even need to videotape his days to achieve more).

This overabundance of available storage capacity makes it easy for us to shift our behavioral default regarding external memory from forgetting to remembering. We save different versions of the documents we are working on to our hard disks. And store images and music files, on the assumption that perhaps some day we might need them. Storing information has become fantastically convenient, but it's more than convenience that induces us to preserve. The truth is that the economics of storage have made forgetting brutally expensive. Consider digital cameras: When you connect your camera to your computer to upload the images you took onto your hard disk, you are usually given a choice. You can either select which images to upload, or have your computer copy automatically all images from your camera. Reassured perhaps by the soothing idea that one can always go through them later and delete the images one does not like, invariably most people choose the latter option. Economically speaking, this makes sense. Assuming it takes only three seconds for a person to look at an image and decide whether to preserve it or not, and that she values her own time at a current average wage, the "cost" of the time alone that it takes to decide exceeds the cost of storage (including having a second copy on a backup device).[18] With such an abundance of cheap storage, it is simply no longer economical to even decide whether to remember or forget. Forgetting—the three seconds it takes to choose—has become too expensive for people to use.

What is true for personal storage applies equally to corporate storage. Companywide data warehouses preserve and keep accessible inordinate amounts of information, on business transactions as well as external and internal communications. E-mails are being preserved, and with the spread of mobile messaging devices companies store instant messages as well. Some of it can actually be damning for the company, as Microsoft discovered during antitrust proceedings against it, when government lawyers forced it to hand over millions of internal mails. The situation is quite similar in large public organizations. When Bill Clinton introduced e-mail to the White House, he had little idea that years later as part of Kenneth Starr's relentless investigations into Clinton's personal and intimate activities, some of the e-mails sent by his staffers would resurface. In a telling reversal of policies, George W. Bush ordered his White House staff to use e-mail much more discriminately, and his administration later conceded that electronic records had been (conveniently some say) deleted from servers.[19] Other public officials, including 2008 vice presidential candidate and Alaska governor Sarah Palin have used private e-mail accounts to circumvent recordkeeping requirements.[20] Much additional information gets lost over time not because of equipment failure, but because of software incompatibilities, or bad data management. For example, as *The New York Times* reports, at NASA, 93 percent of 40 surveyed top officials failed to preserve their e-mails appropriately, and thus violated federal record-keeping requirements.[21] Digital memory provides a means for cheap and reliable storage, but without having proper data management procedures, including frequent and reliable backups in place, the benefits of digital storage cannot be reaped fully. And unlike the cost of hard disk storage space, as experts point out, these data management costs do not get halved every eighteen to twenty-four months.[22] But even keeping these limitations in mind, it is obvious that not just individuals, but private as well as public organizations, too, experience the consequences of permanent comprehensive memory.

In 1996/97, Hotmail and Yahoo! Mail debuted, offering free e-mail accounts to anybody. With that offer came a couple of megabytes of free disk space to store incoming e-mails. Millions signed up within a few months. By early 2000, photo-sharing services began offering similar deals, letting users upload and share digital photos gratis. The hallmark of most of these ad-financed services was free limited disk space on central servers, in line with storage cost declines. On April 1, 2004 (no April fool's joke!), Google stunned the competition by offering a free e-mail account with one gigabyte (a thousand megabytes) of storage capacity. This was orders of magnitude more than what their closest competitors offered. One gigabyte of hard disk at that time cost Google a couple of dollars, to which one needs to add data management, electricity, backup, and bandwidth costs. Upping the ante further, Google announced that it would increase storage for users every minute of every day into the future. By early 2009, the per-user free space had grown more than seven-fold to 7.3 gigabytes (there is a storage size counter on the Google Mail's web page).[23] The goal, according to Google is "free storage so you'll never need to delete another message." Yahoo! countered with mail accounts that offer its users *unlimited* e-mail storage space.

Google, of course, not only stores e-mails for users. It also crawls the Web, creating a huge searchable index of web pages (that's how Google became famous), and taking snapshots of pages on the way (so that users can look at "cached" copies if the original web page does not work). In addition, as I mentioned, Google saves every search query, together with every search result that a user clicks on. That requires a huge storage capacity, as Google reportedly handles a billion search queries a day.[24] To achieve such a feat, companies like Google run hundreds of thousands of hard disks in huge server farms. While keeping specifics secret, Google is said to operate (at the very least) half a million servers with up to a million hard disks, each of which has a capacity in excess of 100 gigabytes, providing a total storage capacity of perhaps 100,000 terabytes (million megabytes) of data.

This is a mind-boggling amount of storage space, but the pure hard disk acquisition cost—perhaps around a few hundred million dollars—is actually not *that* dramatic. Plummeting storage prices are one reason, large volume purchases another. An important, but overlooked third reason is that Google has shunned supposedly more reliable, yet more expensive hard disks and instead opted for off-the-shelf cheap consumer drives. It made sense; careful studies of over a hundred thousand such hard disks showed these drives to be highly reliable—not as reliable as their manufacturers advertised, but still failing extremely rarely.[25] An average hard disk works flawlessly for about 300,000 hours before failing. Considering that an entire year has less than 9,000 hours, this represents more than thirty-three years of continuous operation. Put differently, the chance that both an off-the-shelf cheap hard disk and similar backup disk fail in the same year is less than one in a thousand—quite a low probability. These results also imply that the hundreds of millions of off-the-shelf hard disks used by consumers around the world are not only cheap, but also surprisingly reliable storage devices of information.[26]

Experts suggest that the trend of cheaper storage is going to continue into the second decade of the twenty-first century. Companies around the world are working feverishly on the next generation of digital storage devices. In 2007, hard disk manufacturer Fujitsu announced that they had achieved a hard disk storage density of one terabit (a thousand billion information bits) per square inch using a novel storage mechanism on conventional magnetic hard disks. Another line of research investigates nanotechnology to overcome some of the impeding physical limitations of increasing density in magnetic hard drives.[27] Research in solid-state-based memory continues apace as well, with manufacturers pushing chip-based memory as a medium-term alternative to hard disk–based memory, especially in portable devices, like laptop computers. Such silicone-based memory has the additional advantage of significantly lower energy consumption, as no electricity is needed to spin a magnetic platter five thousand times a minute or more—a big advantage in times of high energy prices. In the spring of 2008, Hewlett-Packard announced that it had successfully produced a long-sought circuit element, the memristor, at about 15 nanometers, and would be able to shrink it to 4 nanometers, perhaps a tenth of the size of circuit elements currently in mass production—this could make possible a tenfold increase in solid-state storage capacity.[28] At the same time, IBM announced that their racetrack memory technology, a bit further out, may lead to an increase in memory capacities of 10 to 100 times.[29] These are just three of the many research ideas pursued to increase storage capacity of hard disk and silicone-based memory. In addition, engineers at all large storage manufacturers actively investigate alternative storage methods, including holographic, biological, and quantum computing approaches. The likely medium-term outcome is that storage capacity will continue to double and storage costs to halve about every eighteen to twenty-four months, leaving us with an abundance of cheap digital storage.

Easy Retrieval

Remembering is more than committing information to memory. It includes the ability to retrieve that information later easily and at will. As humans, we are all too familiar with the challenges of information retrieval from our brain's long-term memory. External analog memory, like books, hold huge amounts of information, but finding a particular piece of information in it is difficult and time-consuming. Much of the latent value of stored information remains trapped, unlikely to be utilized. Even though we may have stored it, analog information that cannot be retrieved easily in practical terms is no different from having been forgotten. In contrast, retrieval from digital memory is vastly easier, cheaper, and swifter: a few words in the search box, a click, and within a few seconds a list of matching information is retrieved and presented in neatly formatted lists. Such trouble-free retrieval greatly enhances the value of information.

To be sure, humans have always tried to make information retrieval easier and less cumbersome, but they faced significant hurdles. Take written information. The switch from tablets and scrolls to bound books helped in keeping information together, and certainly improved accessibility, but it did not revolutionize retrieval. Similarly, libraries helped amass information, but didn't do as much in tracking it down. Only well into the second millennium, when workable indices of book collections (initially perhaps developed out of the extensive organization into subdivisions, later chapters and verses of Hebrew and Christian scriptures) became common, were librarians able to locate a book based on title and author.[30] It took centuries of refinement to develop standardized book cataloguing and shelving techniques, as part of the rise of the modern library. The subject index, an alphabetic list of words used in a book (without page numbers!), was introduced in the thirteenth century and spread quickly.[31] It helped a person choose the appropriate volume based on the particular subject area one wanted to know more about. But creating such an index for each book was time-consuming and did little to ease finding the right passage *within* a book. It took another couple of centuries for page numbers—a prerequisite for pinpointing specific information within a book—to emerge in the 1500s, well into the printing revolution. Only when subject index and page numbers were combined was the equivalent of a modern book index achieved, completing the foundations of information retrieval in a large corpus of text.[32]

The rise of businesses and the state made necessary methods of filing and retrieving written documents with ease and precision. Filing systems were devised that mimicked the two-stage system in book libraries: files were placed in filing cabinets, with each file sorted by name, date, or similar criteria. Such systems made timely retrieval possible but required significant overhead: documents had to be meticulously filed—otherwise they might be lost forever; and the organization of the filing system had to be set up with great care since it could hardly be changed later.

Being conversant in knowing how to file and retrieve analog information (from documents to books) became a sought-after quality among information workers, and organizations spent substantial amounts building and maintaining the tools (indexes, catalogues) necessary for information retrieval. By the end of the analog age, retrieval had come a long way. Information could be retrieved from libraries using a combination of book catalogues and subject indices. But it was a tedious task, costly, time-consuming, and fraught with imprecision, as subject catalogues only contained the most important subject terms for each book, and subject indices in books depended on the precision of authors and editors. Moreover, such retrieval systems required nontrivial resources, perhaps available to organizations but rarely to individuals, or at least not at the same level. Consequently, most of the personal information we collect— sketches and paintings, photographs and self-made videos, cassettes with personal recordings, diary entries, notebooks, scrapbooks, as well as official documents, bank statements, and contracts—we do not keep as neatly organized, catalogued, and indexed as the public library does for its collections. Instead, we use a plethora of different systems, which could even include the proverbial shoebox.

The underlying reason for these challenges in information retrieval is the sequential organization of most analog information storage: without additional cues, one has to page through or perhaps even read an entire book to find a particular part; without a clearly defined filing system, one must browse through document after document, page after page, photo after photo. Audiocassettes and videotapes are similarly sequential. If one wants to find a particular scene, watching (perhaps with faster speed) is the only option. The standard recipe to ease these challenges has been to create and maintain separate retrieval tools that permit more pinpointed access: catalogues to identify the appropriate book or file; subject index and pagination to locate the relevant passage in a book; notation of a videotape's topic and content on its outside, along with a list of scenes and timestamps to find a desired scene. But such retrieval tools are inflexible, complex, and require constant and meticulous maintenance.

This all has changed in the digital age, though it did not happen overnight. Although software is malleable, and digital information processing has few inherent constraints, the humans designing the first generations of digital systems were caught up in real-world metaphors of information organization. Thus, early file systems for digital computers replicated the core elements of a library's book catalogue by keeping track of what digital files were stored where. In parallel, software engineers developed methods to organize information within files for easy retrieval. They were helped by the rise of the hard disk, which unlike most analog storage devices permits direct-access nonsequential information retrieval. By the late 1960s, British IBM engineer Ted Codd formulated the theoretical concepts of what he called relational databases—essentially information organized in tables, with rows of related information combined in a record, and columns of similarly structured data (like name, date, reference number, and so on). An individual record could be retrieved using identifiers called keys, but unlike an analog catalogue, these keys were flexible. Keys could be added later if one wanted to search and retrieve records using information (in the case of a book catalogue, for example, "publication date") that had not been made a key before. With such relational databases, conventional analog card catalogues in libraries could be replaced with much more versatile electronic versions. Records of books could be retrieved not just by the author's name or title, but also fragments of name or title, as well as other information like publisher, subject keywords, or even a combination thereof.

Initially, expensive digital storage was used judiciously as primary information storage. As costs for digital storage plummeted, more and more information became digitized, fueling demand for better information retrieval tools. In the United States in the 1970s, Lexis and Westlaw, for example, made available to their customers huge databases with the full text of tens of thousands of court decisions, but these could only be retrieved using a limited set of keys. Customers, however, wanted to find relevant decisions by searching for words in the text of the decision, not just the case name, docket number, date, and a few subject words that had been indexed. The solution was to make searchable every word of every document in the database. Such full-text searches still require input of the precise words or terms and so it is no surefire recipe of finding the desired information, but it is eminently easier and more powerful than a search that is restricted to a small number of predefined search keys.

At first, full-text indexing and searches were used by large providers of information databases, but by the beginning of the twenty-first century it had become a standard feature of all major PC operating systems, bringing the power of pinpoint information retrieval to people's desktops. At the same time, digital devices became capable of more or less automatically generating and managing file metadata (data about a digital file associated with the file) much beyond well-known categories like name or creation date. For example, digital cameras store automatically with each photo a long list of metadata, like aperture, shutter speed, focal length, date, and time of the shot. This data is preserved when the image file is copied onto a hard disk and can then be used to search and retrieve distinct image files. Users can add metadata themselves. A growing number of digital cameras (particularly in cell phones) append the geo-location—the longitude and latitude—of each photo shot to the set of metadata, helping us humans later identify where a picture was taken.

The latest development is a seamless convergence of the modern elements of index, search, and retrieval that obliterates the old distinction between searching on the file level (akin to searching in a book catalogue), and searching within a file (searching for a passage within a book). Such convergent digital information retrieval functions through one simple integrated interface; information is searched and retrieved at all levels, and presented almost momentarily in a visually consistent manner, irrespective of the underlying information format. This is the easy retrieval we are familiar with on both our desktop PCs—whether through Microsoft Search or Apple Spotlight—and the Internet through search engines, like Google's beautifully simple yet powerful retrieval interface.

The difference to the analog age is striking: through easy retrieval, vast amounts of information—hundreds of gigabytes—are no longer an endless sea of bits in which we risk to drown, but a powerful, versatile, and fast extension of our human memory.

However, there is another less obvious and perhaps more troubling dimension to easy retrieval. As the new digital retrieval tools overcome the sequential nature of conventional analog storage, search times are much shortened, but as the results show up on our computer screens, they have been shed of much of their context. In contrast, going through a conventional file sequentially provides quite a bit of context. It may help one to understand how a situation evolved over time, and add background and circumstantial information that is largely missing from an information snippet directly accessed through digital retrieval. Much of the ordering structures used by digital retrieval disregard such context.

Such decontextualization is not a phenomenon only of the digital age. University of California Irvine professor Simon Cole has explained persuasively how contextual fingerprints taken by law enforcement have become decontextualized, reduced to abstract numerical features to facilitate comparison, search, and retrieval, resulting in unflattering increases in fingerprint misidentifications.[33] At other times, the original context not only gets dropped but replaced with a different one. For example, as UCLA geography professor Michael Curry has shown, the system of postal addresses, including postal codes, first shifted from one that was based on a particular context of place to a more abstract one based on geographic position. Marketing companies then took this decontextualized geographic data (e.g., ZIP codes), and linked it to demographic information, thereby recontextualizing the information. Thus, for example, if today we hear of ZIP code 90210, it immediately conjures images not of a place in California, but of the rich and famous.[34]

Digital tools have been hastening this transition to systems of abstract ordering and categorization, stripping away original context. Such clear and abstract ordering categories were easier to implement and reflect in digital retrieval, even though such an approach may have impoverished the results. Lately, software engineers around the world have been rushing to amend our digital tools to enable a modicum of (re)contextualization—for example, by using metadata and tags. But for now, we'll have to contend with phenomenally cheap, widespread, and easy-to-use retrieval tools, as well as the inherent, but rarely realized, weakness in the de- and recontextualized results they produce.

Global Reach

Cheap storage and easy retrieval transform digital memory into a powerful tool that extends human remembering. The person wanting to access the stored information, however, still has to be at its physical location. Global digital networks eliminate this constraint of physical presence. To retrieve information from a database connected to a global digital network, one needs only be connected to that network. This fundamentally alters the economics of search and retrieval, as time and cost of traveling in person to a particular database to access it are replaced by (the much lower) communication expenses over the network.

Commercial database vendors were the first to grasp the potential of global digital networks for information access. In the 1970s and 1980s they connected their information databases to global digital networks, opening them up to new markets. These additional, mostly commercial customers would have never traveled from afar to search and retrieve a database, but found value in doing so through much more convenient and affordable remote access. The Internet only deepened this change. Communication costs for remote access were reduced to negligible amounts, broadening the potential customer base from commercial entities to all users. As costs came down, the richness of information accessible through the global network increased, too—from simple text to high-definition video. Instead of traveling across the Atlantic to access information only a few decades earlier, one can now do the same from the comfort of one's office or home at a trifling cost, and do so quickly, irrespective of opening hours, all day, seven days a week.

In the late 1990s, the vast majority of people even in industrialized nations connected to the Internet through dialup connections transmitting, at best, perhaps 7,000 bytes per second. By 2008, more than 330 million people had broadband connections, receiving in excess of 100,000 bytes per second.[35] To achieve such a staggering 15-fold increase, connection speeds must have doubled roughly every fifteen months, thus outpacing the already phenomenal growth of both processing power and storage capacity. At the same time, monthly connection fees have remained relatively flat, resulting in an equally amazing decrease in communication costs. Moreover, because almost all broadband connections are offered for a flat monthly fee, they create a further economic incentive for users to maximize utilization of the network.

Three drivers have facilitated this development. The first is the packet-switched structure of the Internet. Unlike the telephone system, which directly connects two communication parties, information on the Internet travels in small information packets that find the fastest way from sender to recipient independently of each other. This leads to a much better utilization of the available network infrastructure. Second, a huge amount of fiber optic cable ideal for broadband connections has been laid. During 1999, for example, it was estimated that 4,000 miles of fiber optic cable were laid in the United States—every day.[36] In the wake of the burst of the first dot-com and telecom bubble, this resulted in excess capacity, with up to 95 percent of the laid long-distance fiber optic cables initially not "lit," (i.e., not used).[37] It hurt investors badly, but has made possible fast subsequent growth. As investors see Web 2.0 services stimulate fast broadband growth, a substantial amount of money is pouring into further broadband infrastructure improvements. Third, technology facilitates retrofitting existing infrastructure to meet demand increases without physically laying new cable. Light is used to transmit information through fiber optic cable. If one can shorten the time a light impulse representing an information bit takes, one can increase the transmission speed through existing cable. Reducing wavelength as well as sending multiple polarized light pulses through the same cable at the same time yields speed advances of another order of magnitude. Similarly, transmission speeds through existing copper cables have been drastically increased by refined versions of original DSL technology. At least in the medium term, it is likely that access speeds will continue to increase at a stable cost. Of course, such an abundance of affordable bandwidth to access information on the global network does not imply that it is available to everybody. People in developing nations, as well as in rural areas of the industrialized world continue to be left out, or connected at much lower speeds and higher cost—requiring important policy considerations in many societies.

Yet, for hundreds of millions of people around the world, information access no longer depends on physical location or the ability to pay (nontrivial) communication costs, but only on policies and fees charged by information providers. The consequences are far-reaching: Digital information connected to the global network suddenly becomes valuable, while information that is not connected is no different from information that has simply been forgotten. Digitization combined with comprehensive and cheap storage, easy retrieval, and global reach enables information to be affordably kept available and reachable forever.

Of course, information we store on our individual hard disks is not automatically accessible for the rest of the world even if we ourselves are connected to the Internet. Commercial providers of information, one may argue, but not individuals, offer their digital treasures online. Even if that view was true (and we'll discuss the merits of it in a minute), our shared digital memory would still expand significantly, and make forgetting harder. The reason is information economics. Unlike the production of most physical goods—think of shoes or a wooden chair—almost the entire cost of information goods is spent on the production of the first piece, while the making of subsequent copies incurs a relatively negligible cost. Take a blockbuster movie: creating it is the expensive and difficult part, producing copies to show in theaters is comparatively trivial. The same is true for books, music,—and for information databases. Consequently, there is a strong incentive for anyone with an information database to utilize it in as many ways as possible. Incremental costs are negligible compared to potential additional revenues. This pushes collectors of information to have their information treasures accessed by many others.

By the same token, commercial information vendors have a strong economic incentive to bundle even unrelated information databases together. This may sound unintuitive. Why should it make sense to offer customers combined access to, say, a database of legal precedents together with a database containing the full text of leading newspapers and newswires? At least at first glance, lawyers searching for precedents and journalists researching stories seem to have little in common. But such a strategy is, as professors Yanos Bakos and Erik Brynjolfsson have shown, eminently sensible, and preferable to selling separately access to individual information sets.[38] Their reasoning is straightforward: Information vendors do not know exactly what information their customers want, and the smaller and more focused an information set is, the harder it is to know whether it meets customer preferences. A larger bundle of information databases on the other hand will satisfy a larger set of customer preferences, and appeal to a broader market. Because of the economics of information production, higher potential revenues are not offset completely by higher costs of adding information sets to one's information bundle. This leads those that have information to grant licenses to commercial information vendors, and for these vendors to approach third-party information providers for a license in order to enhance the information bundles they offer. The result—a combined push and pull in information markets—contributes to the reversal of forgetting that we humans have been used to for millennia.

But let's revisit the premise that only commercial vendors offer information online, not individuals. Technically, there is nothing that prevents individuals from offering their information online. The Internet is a digital network, in which every participant can be a sender as well as a receiver. Obliterating the traditional distinction between information seekers and information providers, between readers and authors, has been a much-discussed quality since the early days of the Internet. At first, its practical effect was limited, as most people accessed the Internet through slow dialup connections and information storage was expensive but over the years this has changed. More and more people around the world connect to the Internet through broadband connections that can accommodate high information transfer rates, and flat connection fees create an incentive to utilize that fat information pipe, including sharing information with others.[39] To limit the potential strain on the network, some broadband providers prohibit users from operating web servers, and thus from serving their information treasures as simple web pages to the rest of the world. But specialized web-hosting companies offer space on their web servers for a monthly fee (due to severe competition in 2008, 10 dollars a month would get one 50 gigabytes of web space and 1,000 gigabytes of monthly information transfer volume, enough to host 25 million pages of text, tens of thousands of digital photos, or a dozen high-definition videos). Another way to overcome these limitations is to use peer-to-peer file sharing software for music and videos, as well as any other file. They work well, as tens of millions of users have discovered, and broadband providers have a harder time to interdict them technically. Moreover, because nowadays peer-to-peer information sharing has become such a widespread phenomenon, broadband users simply expect their providers not to constrain their information sharing behavior.

Individuals can also easily share information with others using a recent wave of dot-com companies. Often described as providers of Web 2.0 services, they aim at facilitating the creation of online communities based on mutually shared information. Flickr and YouTube are examples of such services. Anyone can upload images and videos and have them stored and made accessible to the rest of the world for free. This way, sharing information becomes incredibly easy. The companies behind Flickr and YouTube—Yahoo! and Google—are well-known online information providers. Cheap storage and the global spread of broadband access is one reason why they can afford offering these services for free. They also hope to capitalize eventually on the social networks, the online communities that are forming. Most importantly perhaps, it helps them reassert their role as preeminent entry gates into the global information sea. Hundreds of millions of users around the world have embraced these and similar services—think of Facebook, MySpace, or Twitter. For them, the Internet has changed profoundly since 2000. As I suggested in the introduction, before 2000 it was a tool to *access* information, today it is also a tool to *share* information. This implies a shift from passive recipient to active contributor, quite similar to what digitization has done for producing and consuming information itself.

Of course, Gordon Bell, the software engineer who has captured much of his professional life on digital memory, emphatically insists he is in charge of whether and how he makes his information available to others. Bell himself has decided to not let others peek into his information treasures. His lifeblog project, he explains, is about helping *him* remember, not giving others access to his files: "A lot of people put their lives on the Web. I'm not an advocate of that. [Lifeblogging] was built to be entirely personal, to aid the individual."[40] His view may be admirable but, as he concedes, it is not representative of current Internet users. As I have mentioned, two out of three teenagers in the United States use the Internet to create and share information with others.[41] This large and growing portion of the user population has internalized the culture of information bricolage. They enjoy the vast benefits of what economists have termed network externalities—every new user joining to share information increases the value for all existing users. Still, one could argue, even though users see the Internet as a global tool for information sharing among individuals, users choose deliberately to permit others to access information through the global network. If they do not or no longer want to grant others access, they can do so. After all, the beauty of digitized information is that erasing it is as easy as clicking "delete." This may sound true at first, but it rarely is for at least two reasons, both of which are fundamental to how information networks operate.

The first is that once one has shared information, one has essentially lost control over it. If I let others access my information, I have to trust that they do not use it contrary to my wishes. If they break my trust, there is little I can do about it. And I am not thinking about some technically sophisticated hacker breaking into my computer and stealing information. That, too, happens to many unsuspecting users. And not always does it require technical sophistication, as celebrity Paris Hilton discovered in 2005. She used a feature of her mobile phone provider to back up the information stored in her handset onto the provider's central computer. Access to the stored information required a password, or—for those users who had forgotten their password—the name of their favorite pet. As a celebrity, the name of Hilton's pet dog was public knowledge. A 17-year-old teenager used that information to get access to Paris Hilton's backup of her phone contacts and digital images, and then made that information accessible to the rest of the world through peer-to-peer file-sharing networks.[42] The teenager was later caught and convicted for his involvement in another case. But the damage was done. It wasn't just Paris Hilton whose personal information was exposed; everybody on her phone contact list had their (often unlisted) phone number revealed. Many had to have their phone numbers changed, in turn requiring them to inform their friends, colleagues, and business partners. All these individuals had lost control over their phone numbers not when the teenager accessed Hilton's files, but much earlier, when they entrusted Hilton with it.

This may sound like an exceptional case—and the phone provider quickly patched the weakness—but as the BBC reported, over a 100 million unsuspecting users of social networking site Facebook may be equally at risk having their personal information exposed.[43] Or think of much simpler acts of information misuse that happen millions of times every day: We tell a friend or colleague something valuable, perhaps a good idea, a fact, or just gossip, and he passes on that information to a third party. We are not asked for our consent—in fact, we don't even know. We find out only accidentally if at all. In the analog age, the danger was somewhat mitigated by one's capacity to spread information. Few of us commanded a printing press or ran a television show. Yet, even if such information spreads slowly or only to a few recipients, it can be quite damaging. This is why we do not tell everything to everybody, and make deliberate choices whom to tell what and when. Moreover, because most such individual communication in analog times was oral, in some situations one could pretend it was all a big "misunderstanding," and perhaps eventually the incident would be forgotten. In the digital world, the situation is more complex. Through global reach, information can spread much more quickly and over a much wider area than before. Digitization makes copying and sharing easier and faster, and thus less controllable, and its growing media-richness (audio and video in addition to text) makes it less deniable. Furthermore, because the digital copy is a perfect replica of the original, tracking the flow of information to a possible leak or identifying its origin is difficult. In the digital age, it has become very hard to recall information, and to stop others from sharing it, especially once a piece of information has begun to spread beyond narrow geographic and demographic confines.

The second reason why we may no longer be the masters of our information treasures is that each online interaction itself—even if one does not share files—is information about oneself that one's interaction partner(s) now have, and can possibly share with others. If I order a book at Amazon.com, I leave behind an information trail that Amazon uses—among other things—to recommend books to me. Perhaps one would expect that. But the same is true when I only browse Amazon's online store, even though I have not explicitly told Amazon to watch my browsing habits. They do it anyway. At times, I benefit from it when Amazon presents a selection of products that might appeal to me based on the information trail I have left behind. Most online retailers do the same, as do companies offering web-based e-mail, social networking, and information sharing. And Internet search companies watch carefully what users search for. Some may counter that we do not have to shop or buy online, to send or receive e-mails, blog, engage in virtual worlds, use search engines, or allow cookies. It still requires our participation for others to record our digital traces. But that argument is patently disingenuous, for at least two reasons. First, often users do not know that their digital activities are being recorded and committed to digital memory—from browsing at Amazon to drafting e-mails on Google mail. Similarly, users may enjoy the auto-complete function in their web browsers when typing in a web address or filling in an order form, but its unclear that they comprehend that this implies that their web browsers keep a record of their activities. Or users may like that they can now quickly search their hard disks using powerful full-text indexing and retrieval, but might not understand that this is because whatever they store on their PCs is being indexed by default. Switching off these defaults of remembering is complex, and in many cases impossible. Second, even if users would have perfect knowledge of the continuous and comprehensive digital remembering of their activities, the only easy remedy available to them would be to turn into digital recluses and abstain from taking part in online interactions, and many offline ones as well. This is because every communication with the world produces a piece of information. As communication theorist Paul Watzlawick once noted in a more general context, "one cannot not communicate." [44] And insofar as such communication is using any digital devices along the way, chances are it will be added to our digital shadows.

Add to this the widespread digital mixing and meshing of various information sources to create anything from the utterly banal to the incredible creative, from funny to thoughtful, from simple to complex. With our personal computers as general-purpose information processors, our hard disks offering ample storage, and sophisticated editing and mixing software becoming affordable as well as easy to use, cutting, editing, adding, and recombining digital information is now available to many millions of users. But the creators of these new cultural products take information out of its existing context, and associate a new context with it. Russian Goblin edits—the redubbing of blockbuster movies that I mentioned—are so remarkable precisely because replacing familiar dialogues with a new one recontextualizes movies we thought we knew, and gives them a very different take. Music sampling—reusing snippets of well-known music as elements of a new recording—is a similar concept.

Kansas State University professor Michael Wesch's video *Web 2.0*—a beautiful and eloquent piece explaining the rise of the digital bricolage—offers an intriguing example. In early 2007, he posted it on YouTube. Within weeks, millions had watched the movie. That would not have been possible in the analog age. But more importantly, in the weeks afterwards, others took Wesch's video, translated it into different languages, created response videos disputing some of Wesch's assumptions but mimicking his artistic style, or even completely remixed Wesch's original work. Wesch's video became famous, not only because millions watched it, but because many took it as a departure point for their own works. The story of Wesch's video and what it triggered is familiar to those that follow what has been happening on YouTube and the numerous other information sharing sites. The ability to actively create by recombining existing information of others rather than just passively own prerecorded content has unleashed tremendous creative potential. Incidentally, it has also caused shared digital information to become de- and recontextualized without the control of the

original creator. As I have described earlier, information retrieval already causes information to become de- and recontextualized because pieces of information are retrieved without
their accompanying contexts and presented in a new context of
search results. With enough time and effort, though, one often
could track retrieved results back to the information source,
and thus experience them in the original context. It's like finding a passage in a book using the index—a person might not
grasp the full context by reading just a sentence or a page, but
if sufficiently important, they can then read the chapter or even
the entire book. With digital bricolages, this is no longer possible, since the information pieces that make up the bricolage are
severed from their original context, without a way to trace
them back. If a photo is used in a slideshow, a sentence taken
from somebody's novel, or a few notes of music plucked from a
song, in a digital bricolage we have no reference to find the
"original," and thus the context in which the photo was originally taken, the sentence written, or the musical notes composed and played. If nothing else, this heightens the danger of
misinterpretation.

Gordon Bell thus may not reveal what he has stored in his
digital notes, but if he partakes in the information creating-
and-sharing culture of the Internet, he will discover that over
time much of the content of his digital notes may find their way
into the hands of others. At times, he may deliberately share information, trusting his recipients. At other times, he may be
unaware or have forgotten that information generated by his
online interactions is stored and used by others. Do not get me
wrong: sharing information is often hugely beneficial and perfect informational control was an illusion even in analog times
except for the most ardent recluse. But the fact is that in the
digital age, our capacity as individuals to control information is
vastly reduced.

No doubt, the technological breakthroughs over the last six decades have facilitated the storing and recalling of an ever-increasing amount of information. And the greatly diminished cost for processing, storing, and recalling digital information acts as a strong and sustained incentive for individuals to use the new tools en masse. Perhaps equally important is how digital memory offers us a strategy of continuity and preservation to transcend our individual mortality. It lets us leave behind traces, as philosopher Robert Nozick suggested, thereby implying that "a person's life had a certain meaning."[45] By using digital memory, our thoughts, emotions, and experiences may not be lost once we pass away but remain to be used by posterity. Through them we live on, and escape being forgotten. As fertility rates plummet in modern societies, our desire to preserve the memory of our lives outside of the traditional context of intergenerational sharing may get stronger. It is a very human strategy to ensure that we haven't lived in vain, that we aren't quickly forgotten after our deaths as if we've never lived.

With widespread digitization, more and more information is being translated in a common binary code. Through cheap storage technology, keeping digital information has become not only affordable, but frequently cheaper than taking the time to selectively delete some of it. Easy retrieval tools have enabled us to utilize our huge digital information treasures like never before. And global reach through fast and affordable digital networks has not only made possible remote access to these information treasures, but also facilitated a culture of creation, bricolage, and sharing in which we have abandoned traditional forms of information control. And with more humans looking for strategies of transcending mortality other than procreating, the human demand for more comprehensive digital memory will continue to rise. The result is a world that is set to remember, and that has little if any incentive to forget.

CHAPTER IV

Of Power and Time— Consequences of the Demise of Forgetting

H umans yearn to remember, although they mostly forget. To lighten this biological limitation, we have developed tools—from books to videos—that function as external memory for us. These tools have proved tremendously helpful, as they have made remembering easier and accessible to many more people than ever before. But until a few decades ago, these tools did not unsettle the balance between remembering and forgetting: to remember was the exception; to forget, the default.

In the digital age, this balance has been altered fundamentally. Digitization, the theoretical underpinning of the digital revolution, has led to cheap digital storage, easy retrieval, and global access. Today, forgetting has become costly and difficult, while remembering is inexpensive and easy. With the help of digital tools we—individually and as a society—have begun to unlearn forgetting, to erase from our daily practices one of the most fundamental behavioral mechanisms of humankind.

This could be reason for celebration. After all, haven't humans tried for millennia to overcome the straightjacket of biological forgetting and failing human memories? Our vast and accessible digital memories offer innumerable benefits, from increased accuracy and improved efficiency to the promise to help us transcend human mortality.

For example, comprehensive digital medical files that include information of a person's rare allergy from many years ago may prove life-saving particularly when compared with the alternatives, such as a doctor's imperfect memory, or her handwritten notes, which may be hard to decipher after many years. Similarly, CCTV recordings and airplane black boxes offer more accurate information to accident investigators than a witness' brain reconstructing the past. The additional efficiency achieved through comprehensive and easy remembering is equally remarkable. Faster and wider dissemination of information (whether scientific results or raw data) may lead to accelerated innovation and economic growth. A more exacting digital memory may aid businesses in designing and producing more precisely the goods people prefer, and in marketing them to better-defined target groups, thus sparing them, consumers, and the environment from millions of tons of unwanted marketing and advertisement material (although consumers are uncomfortable being targeted that way).[1]

Economists have long argued that better information increases efficiency.[2] eBay's system of rating buyers and sellers is a case in point. It functions as a comprehensive external memory for all market participants, providing potential future transaction partners with a valuable signal about their counterpart's past behavior.[3] But the benefits of digital remembering are not limited to efficiency gains in market transactions. They also extend to broader societal concerns, as well as to cases where information had been recorded in the past but was not easily accessible, and thus could not be used by others. For example, the New York City Department of Health and Mental Hygiene conducts hygiene audits at restaurants in the city. Once this information was made available online, it had immediate reputational consequences for restaurants found to have questionable food hygiene practices.[4] Similarly, for years the U.S. Environmental Protection Agency required polluters to self-report storage and emission of toxins and pollutants. The information was dutifully entered into a digital database together with related information, but that was it. Only when the EPA made the database accessible online, and combined it with an easy-to-use online map, could consumers (rather than researchers) check easily their neighborhood for pollution sources, prompting them to mount local campaigns for a cleanup.[5] Moreover, the EPA, much like the New York City Department of Health and Mental Hygiene, permitted third parties, including NGOs, to access the database and combine the retrieved information with their own information, maps, and demographics. As Mary Graham has shown, such public shaming does have an impact on industry behavior.[6] Without a comprehensive digital memory, neither the transactional reputation on eBay nor the environmental reputation through the New York City Department of Health and Mental Hygiene or the EPA would work well.

Digital memory may also improve the precision of government decision-making on the individual as well as the societal level. When individuals apply for a government service, comprehensive digital memory may lead government agencies to render more accurate decisions.[7] On a societal level, such accessible digital memory aids in forecasting general trends and societywide development, enabling policy makers to adjust policies before problems have gotten out of hand. In addition, the electorate can tap into digital memory to see whether and how their political representatives keep their promises.[8]

These are some of the frequently suggested reasons why the shift from human forgetting to perfect remembering ought to be comforting rather than troubling. But even just a more detailed look at the supposed benefits of comprehensive digital memory reveals a more complex picture. For example, reputation on eBay is not as accurate a reflection of transactional satisfaction as the economic argument of signaling suggests. Researchers have discovered that sellers on eBay strategically time their rating of the buyer. Many of them rate buyers highly even before the transaction has concluded (when they would have the relevant information to rate buyers)—not because they are satisfied with a transaction, but because they hope to elicit an equally good rating in return.[9] It is but one of the many ways in which eBay's customers have been trying to influence eBay's digital memory of transactional reputation.[10] By the spring of 2008, the widespread behavior of gaming reputation memory led eBay to a dramatic reversal of its information policy. It announced that sellers would no longer be able to rate buyers except positively.[11] Whereas, since its beginning, eBay's trademark had been to remember reputation, it has now introduced the deliberate forgetting of bad experiences.

Or take the EPA's helpful web site combining geographic and pollution information. It worked well until the EPA realized that its comprehensive digital memory of emission and toxic waste storage in the U.S. might offer an invaluable tool to terrorists searching for suitable targets. As the EPA found out, digital memory that is beneficial in one context (and for one purpose) may prove to be harmful in another. As a consequence, the EPA's full and open access to its Envirofacts database was axed quickly.[12]

Digital memory may offer important benefits, but—as these two cases demonstrate—not necessarily all the time. In some instances, people may succeed in gaming or otherwise altering digital memory to further their purposes. Other times, accessible digital memory may enhance short-term efficiency but expose individuals or society to potentially harmful consequences.[13] The example of digital medical records illustrates another potential difficulty: Suppose one's entire medical information was in some accessible digital storage. How should it be organized to ensure a doctor accessing it could quickly locate the pertinent pieces while ensuring potentially lifesaving cross-references between information? How would information added over a person's lifetime be interpreted given that the contexts in which the individual information bits had been collected over the years and decades varied greatly? What one doctor might have thought of as a "troubling response" to a particular therapy or medication, for example, may be described as a "normal reaction" by another, or even by the same person with a couple of years of extra experience.[14] Perfect remembering exposes us to filtering, selection, and interpretation challenges that forgetting has mostly shielded us from. Like eBay and the EPA, our health care providers may discover that the ability to remember everything is not useful all the time.

Let's take stock: comprehensive digital memory fails to realize all the envisioned benefits; sometimes the benefits caused by increased accuracy and efficiency are offset by some economic disadvantage or harm, as the EPA case seems to suggest. But the problem with digital memory is deeper and cannot be reduced easily to a simple cost/benefit analysis. For millennia, human beings have lived in a world of forgetting. Individual behavior, societal mechanisms and processes, and human values have incorporated and reflected that fact. It would be naïve to think that leaving behind such a fundamental part of human nature with the help of digitization and technology would be a painless affair. In numerous ways humans adjust quickly to different environmental conditions, but it takes many generations for fundamental traits of human behavior to get altered or replaced. And even if we were able to cope with this new world of remembering by default and to get through a painful adjustment phase, would we view it as an important advancement, or rather as a terrible curse?

The arguments in favor of remembering focus on the perceived higher quality of digitally remembered information, the efficiencies resulting from utilizing digital memory, and the more transcendental idea of informational immortality that digital memory promises to provide. What is missing from these arguments is the actual impact that supplanting forgetting with remembering has on human beings, and on society as a whole. How will our lives be affected? How will human behavior adjust, and will the result be an improvement over our current situation, or more of a loss instead? A world without forgetting is difficult to predict, but based on available research, stringent analysis, and a modicum of conjecture, we can sketch the contours of the challenge we face. Two terms characterize what truly is at stake: power and time.

Power

"*Knowledge is power*," Sir Francis Bacon wrote four hundred years ago.[15] It is a concept that is deeply rooted in human behavior: acquiring information about what surrounds us helps us survive. In many circumstances, that power is relative, stemming from knowing more than others. From the early days of humankind, special castes, groups, and professions emerged that maintained the perception of unique access to information. They could communicate with the gods, heal illnesses, command spirits, direct armies, advance production, or rule societies. As much as we are curious and like to know what is going on around us, we are just as much consciously *not* sharing all information with everyone.

Keeping information to ourselves to retain information advantages may be culturally acquired, perhaps a consequence of developments of recent decades. Very likely, though, it is much older. When in the sixteenth century the Reformation movement swept across Europe, it broke the Catholic Church's power in part by undermining the Church's role as society's central information intermediary. After Martin Luther, humans could read the Bible themselves rather than having to accept what they were told by somebody "in the know" (and, conversely, sins were confessed directly to God, not to members of the priesthood, thus depriving the Church of important inside knowledge). As a consequence, the power of the Catholic Church eroded, giving secular nation-states a chance to rise. Or take books, for example: When the printing press spread, in many nations book publishers teamed up with governments to establish a system of information control to cement their power. Books would only be printed after approval by government censors. In return, publishers' guilds were granted exclusive privileges to print them.[16] In this light, the first legislative act of granting authors rights in their works (the Copyright Act of 1709) arguably happened because book publishers had become too powerful for Queen Anne.[17] Copyright, Anne's legal invention, promised to break the publishers' might by empowering authors. As professors Robert Keohane and Joseph Nye have explained, people have long understood that the power of information is derived from the ability to control access to it.[18] Of course, not everybody is an author weighing whether to publish their manuscript. But all humans have information about themselves, who they are, where they come from, what they think they may want to share with others—or not share.

The question is to what extent they can control what information others are able to obtain about them.

Physical space has long been an effective antidote to too noisy a neighbor. When the next farm is many miles away, what one does or says is less likely to spread, except intentionally.[19] In cities, on the other hand, one cannot escape being watched by others. The sheer number of people guarantees a certain level of anonymity. As everybody is bombarded with information, most of it drowns in the sea of sensory impressions city life produces. In both cases, individuals remain (at least to an extent) in control of what information about them is available to others. By contrast, in villages and similar communities with little space between each other and too few citizens for the veil of anonymity to work, controlling the flow of one's personal information is much harder. In such circumstances, control over one's information may come from social norms—for example, it might simply be considered inappropriate to read someone's diary.

If all else fails to control information, people have had another, albeit much more costly option: exit. For centuries, moving from one community to another permitted people to restart their lives with a clean slate, as information about them stayed local. Crossing the Atlantic from Europe to the newly founded United States, or into the great Western frontier of the eighteenth and nineteenth centuries let people start from scratch, not just in economic terms, but more importantly in terms of knowledge others had of them.[20] Even moving from one neighborhood to another in a large city might achieve a similar result. In a sense, such moves were akin to declaring information bankruptcy; one could restart once again in control of one's personal information.[21] The costs, though, involved in such a restart through geographic relocation were substantial. Moreover, they depended on one's connections with one's community.

Those with many ties to the community they were leaving behind were exposed to a much higher cost than those that had fewer ties in general, or had ties across disconnected communities so that the exit entailed only a partial rather than a complete severing of links to the outside world.[22]

Over the last few decades, we have witnessed a continuous erosion of an individual's control over their personal information. Companies have significant economic incentives to know more about the preferences of their existing and potential customers, as well as to ensure efficient transactions with them. The welfare state—with its yearning for precise targeting of public services and our society's desire to mitigate many of life's risks—necessitates more personal information to flow from individuals to public and private sector organizations. Digitization combined with cheap information processing and storage has made information flows feasible, both technically and in terms of cost.[23] This has troubled commentators who fear such developments threaten our personal liberty. When the first generation of digital memory spread throughout the United States in the 1960s, academics like Alan Westin and Arthur Miller rose against what they termed an "assault on privacy."[24] The term they used—*information privacy*—stuck, although individuals' desire to retain some control over their information goes much beyond the narrow confines of what we colloquially term privacy.[25]

After four decades of increasing digitization, some believe we have already adapted to the new digital age and understand the risks involved in many of our daily interactions when we share our personal information with others. I am skeptical. We are only good at judging what is obvious to us. Unfortunately, the potential consequences of a default of remembering on our ability to maintain control (and thus have power) over information are rarely transparent. They take place without us noticing much—at first. We may suffer a reduction of control over our information before we realize it. By the same token, others gain in information power from our loss, influencing the circumstances of our future interactions with the world and how we function as a society. Three features of digital memory make this possible.

Accessibility

One way we believe we control the use of our personal information is to decide whether to share it based on recipient and circumstances. For example, we tell our doctor before surgery that we suffer from Hepatitis B, but we won't tell our hairdresser (and we won't even tell a doctor if we meet him socially at the tennis court). We also expect our doctor to use that information only for the very purpose we shared it with him—to properly conduct a medical procedure. Put a bit more abstractly, we link our willingness to share information with others to a particular context and purpose—for which we have weighed the pros and cons of a relative loss in information power. This works well if information is stored in separate disconnected containers, whether they are old-fashioned filing cabinets or a digital database residing on our doctor's computer (disconnected from the rest of the world). That way, even in a digital age it is possible to retain a modicum of control over our personal information by only distributing small subsets of it to different recipients. This strategy of "practical obscurity," [26] however, is undermined by today's widespread ability of others to collect, access, and disseminate the information they have about us, made possible through cheap storage, easy retrieval, and global reach, which are the central elements of comprehensive digital remembering that I described in chapter 3.

For example, when one files a change-of-address form with the U.S. Post Office, one assumes that the post office will only use this information internally to reroute one's mail. That is not the case. The post office also makes accessible change-of-address information to third parties so they (mostly mail catalogue companies) can update their direct mail databases, and ensure that the latest L.L.Bean or Lands End catalogue will follow you wherever you move.[27] Few, if any, of the 40 million Americans who change their address every year know that their new address information is being made accessible this way to third parties. More troubling perhaps is the practice of two thirds of all health insurance companies in the United States to screen health insurance applicants by digitally accessing their prescription histories. Most applicants and even many insurance brokers are unaware of such invasive practices made possible by digital accessibility.[28]

Or take Stacy Snyder: when she put her drunken pirate photo on her MySpace web page, did she really expect her supervisors would notice? Or take photo-sharing web site Flickr. It not only lets users upload photos, but add labels to them (called "tags"). These tags make it possible to search the two billion photos on Flickr. You may not have uploaded any photos that depict you in a compromising situation, but others might have. And with Flickr's image tags, finding the one you are in becomes much easier—for the entire world. That would not have been possible in the analog age. People could have shown a compromising photo of yours to others, but unless you were a public figure it would not have gotten widely distributed. With digital memory, a significant part of one's remaining power over information dissipates and is redistributed to the millions with network access. Developments in video surveillance provide a third case in point. In Britain, millions of CCTV cameras have been installed to prevent crime. But as studies have shown, crime rates dipped only marginally; people discovered police did not have enough staff to browse the recordings these cameras produced. While preserved, information was not accessible. London police are now experimenting with sophisticated software that recognizes distinct logos on clothing to identify its wearer rather than employing less accurate facial recognition, thereby potentially offering law enforcement unprecedented accessibility to the value locked in their video library.[29]

Durability

The second feature of digital remembering that leads to a redistribution of information power is durability. Before digital memory most information, even incriminating items, were forgotten relatively quickly. Special efforts were necessary to ensure remembering, which proved costly and was employed only in special cases. In the Soviet Union, for example, the KGB stamped "хранить вечно" (to be preserved forever) on the dossiers of its political prisoners. The Communist state, the message was, would never forget the identity, beliefs, actions, and words of those that had opposed it, even if that would require extreme efforts.[30] In the digital age, the effort to remember has diminished while value has soared. Google remembers search queries, even though a billion such requests reach it every day. If somebody watches you surf the Web, after a few days that person will have forgotten what you searched for and when. Google will not; its memory of one's search requests is much more durable, as well as accurate.

Combine accessibility and durability, and humans can no longer successfully run away from their past. That past follows them, ready to be tapped into by anyone with an Internet connection.

Comprehensiveness

The third feature is comprehensiveness. With accessibility and durability others can get to personal information stored in different databases that have accumulated over time. But information providers can (and do) go one step further by combining such personal information from different sources and building information-rich dossiers of people, their activities and friends, their preferences, and their beliefs in a matter of seconds. Commercial entities already offer dossiers containing more than a thousand individual data points per person for millions of Americans. Those who want to spend a (relatively small) amount of money can find out about their neighbors, friends, dates, or business partners. The economics of digital remembering make creating personal dossiers cheaper still. Many of us have added our personal profile online, especially in the hope of connecting to a community or a social network. Already search engines that index people are cropping up. They fashion mini-dossiers in real time using information from publicly available sources—for free. One of them, Spock.com is boasting that it has "indexed over 100 million people representing over 1.5 billion data records."[31] Most of these people search engines are still hideously crude and incomplete, but they are getting better quickly. At the same time, traditional Internet search engines are continuously expanding their indexing capabilities from traditional web pages into social networks and thousands of other publicly available databases. It would take a human many dozens of hours to access all of these information sources sequentially and compile a comprehensive dossier, while integrated search engines make it a quick, seamless, easy, and costless affair. But what emerges from such curious queries (even if all of the facts in it were/are perfectly accurate) is not the sought-after encapsulation of one person's present essence, but an oddly artificial composite of our lives, consisting only of information that is available in digital format, leaving out everything else. Moreover, remember the case of Andrew Feldmar, the Canadian psychotherapist who was refused entry to

the United States because a border guard used Google to discover on the Internet that he had taken drugs in the 60s? Until
recently, one could have reasonably expected that information
given to different recipients for different purposes years ago
would remain largely inaccessible to third parties. Of course, my
doctor may play tennis with my hairdresser and coincidentally
tell him my medical record. Such accidental leakages happen,
but for the most part their impact is limited. In an age of digital
remembering, however, these leakages have become the rule
rather than the exception—and the consequences are pervasive.

Comprehensiveness also leads to the danger of incorrect information inferences. Once you have browsed and shopped at
Amazon, you will be presented with book (and other product)
recommendations. Amazon has no crystal ball to read your
mind. Rather they use your browsing and shopping decisions
to search another shopper in their database with similar tastes.
If they have identified one, they recommend what other products that shopper has bought to you, assuming that the purchases you have in common reveal a more general alignment
of preferences. The problem is that such information inferences
are probability based. They tenuously link individuals to certain preferences. The result is a digital and much broadened
version of guilt by association, as inferences based on matching
individual characteristics are used to render judgment.[32]

Most individuals dislike any unexpected and involuntary
loss of control over their information. What happens if the
powerful use their superior bargaining position vis-à-vis others
to gain access to information without having to share their own?
To counter such danger, novelist David Brin has proposed what
he termed "reciprocal transparency"—a principle of sharing
our information with our counterparts only if they recipro-
cate.[33] That way he hopes to overcome imbalances in information power, and help us achieve true information symmetry.

At first look, it sounds like a nifty idea, but it is unclear to me how it could prevent the impulse transactional partners have—as the case of eBay's reputation mechanism so strikingly demonstrates—of gaming the system. Of course, reciprocal transparency may still be beneficial for society, even if it fails to prevent individuals from providing each other with incorrect information. Consider that in the analog age, if one had a dark side, he could hide it. If you can't be good, be careful, is the phrase legal historian Lawrence Friedman uses in his magisterial book on reputation.[34] Wouldn't it therefore be advantageous for society if people couldn't hide their dark sides as easily anymore, if we knew more (or all) about each other? Wouldn't deception be harder if the tight control we maintain over our personal information could be replaced by equal access? Brin's vision is a world in which decentralized reciprocal access to personal information erodes the stranglehold of those that can force (and have forced) their access to information in our society.

Unfortunately, human remembering is not a process of mechanistically retrieving facts from our past, but rather, as Daniel Schacter so eloquently argued, the constant reconstruction of our past based on the present.[35] Or as he puts it "present influences play a much larger role in determining what is remembered than what actually happened in the past."[36] While we are constantly forgetting and reconstructing elements of our past, others employing digital remembering can access the unreconstructed facts. Thus, as the past we remember is constantly (if ever so slightly) changing and evolving, the past captured in digital memory is constant, frozen in time. Likely these two visions will clash—the frozen memory others have about us, and the evolving emerging memory we carry in our minds. Neither is an accurate and complete depiction of what we are. The former is locked in time, the latter our mind's rendition of the past, strongly influenced by who we are in the present. In such a world, would we still resort to human memory, or switch ourselves to digital memory to ensure that others do not know more about us, even when recalling our very own history? And if we all switched from individual human to some external digital remembering, and thus gave up on our ability to see our past through the eyes of who we are in the present, would this not have perverted Brin's very idea of preserving individuals' ability to control information?

Brin's intriguing idea suffers from another weakness. He envisions a world of information symmetries as individuals refuse to unilaterally negotiate away control over their information. But this view implies that the negotiations over "reciprocal transparency" can be conducted on equal footing and without individuals being forced to give more than they receive from powerful transactional partners. That is wishful thinking. Instead of the rosy picture of information symmetry achieved through fair and equal negotiations about information control and access, mighty transaction partners (think of large corporations or government) may employ their power differentials to obtain information advantages. Instead of information reciprocity, what we may witness is an ensuing redistribution of information power from the powerless to the powerful—or to put it in the information privacy context from the surveyed to the surveillant—that often takes place without the explicit consent (or even knowledge) of those from which power is taken. Such information redistribution is deeply troubling in itself (as I will detail in chapter 5) since it amplifies and deepens existing power differentials between the information rich and the information poor. But its long-term effect on how we conceive of our own past is equally troubling: because we continuously (re)construct our past in our memory, over time our own recollection of an interaction will become qualitatively inferior to the digitally stored image the information rich possess of us, thus essentially denying us our own past.

Information privacy experts have long argued that retaining some control over one's information gives a human being the space she needs to define herself. If, as I have suggested, the widespread use of digital remembering leads to a loss of information control, it constricts precisely the freedom to shape one's own identity that these experts have been talking about, except that in a world of digital memory an individual's loss of control over information, and thus their loss of relative information power, may be larger than what the concept of information privacy traditionally entails.

So far, we have looked at how digital remembering alters the balance of information power in a dyadic relationship, and how this causes transactions to take place and under what conditions. Consumers, for example, may pay more for goods and services because of the information differential a well-informed seller utilizing digital memory possesses. Think of a database of worldwide automobile accidents; those renting a car could be charged differently based on their past driving history, which through digital remembering could be made instantly accessible to rental companies. Even if renters knew what information about their driving history the database contained (and could fix erroneous information), they would still have to pay more if the history correctly showed that they had had accidents in the past. The only way to avoid paying extra is something that is no longer possible in this age of digital memory: to forget, or at least unilaterally "reconstruct" one's personal history. If I know, however, that I cannot alter my driving record after the fact, I will drive more carefully to avoid tainting it. If retrospective redemption is unattainable, what remains is prospective caution.

A shift in information power therefore doesn't have consequences just for a particular transaction, whether and under what conditions it takes place, it also has the potential to influence how humans behave. Remember the cases of aspiring teacher Stacy Snyder and psychotherapist Andrew Feldmar? Both said afterwards that in hindsight they would have acted differently. Had they known the consequences they would have self-censored themselves. But there is an important difference between Stacy's and Andrew's case. Stacy Snyder failed to understand the accessibility quality of digital remembering—what is available for one purpose and one recipient may be accessible to somebody else and used for a very different purpose; otherwise, she likely would have not posted the picture on her web page. Here is the important part: that information can be accessed, and for different reasons, by others than the original recipient restrains how Stacy expresses herself—*in general*. If one does not know how one's utterances will be used and by whom, one must assume the worst, namely that any criticism will end up where it will cause the most damage.[37] In a talk with *New York Times* columnist Thomas Friedman, Google CEO Eric Schmidt called this "living with a historical record" and cautioned that people will have to become "much more careful how they talk, how they interact, what they offer of themselves" to others.[38] The implication is clear: the way to avoid exposure is to not criticize. This, however, solidifies the power differential between the surveyed and the surveillant, much like in Bentham's panopticon: Because Stacy Snyder does not know whether her web page is being watched and by whom, she should assume that her supervisor does so all the time, and thus she better behave accordingly—or risk being denied her teacher's certificate.

With respect to the relationship between citizens and the state, we have come to accept that power differences are troubling if they reduce the citizens' ability to openly criticize government with impunity. That is why in the United States the

First Amendment protects the freedom of expression from government intrusion—similar to the Human Rights Convention in Europe and constitutional guarantees of the freedom of expression in many other nations. Where such guarantees are lacking, citizens often are uninterested in public affairs, robust public debate is impoverished, and democracy suffers. The history of dissent in Nazi Germany, as well as in the Soviet Union and its satellites, offers ample and tragic examples. And where dissent was permitted, it was either muted or had to be so artfully camouflaged that it failed to be seen as threatening by those in power.[39]

Yet Stacy did not criticize the state, and it was not government that prevented her from getting a teacher's certificate. Rather it was an expression—the "drunken pirate" photo on her web page—intended for her friends, but received by a private third party (her supervisor).

Perhaps some would argue that this lesson serves her well— that she should grow up and stop posting silly pictures on the Internet. But what behavior can we reasonably expect will keep us out of trouble? I would not have thought that Stacy's picture with pirate hat and mug in hand was so offensive as to prevent her from getting her teacher's certificate; neither had Stacy. But once we realize that information can reach anyone, we'll err on the side of caution, and if in doubt censor ourselves rather than risk incalculable damage. Of course, this is not new. In the analog age, however, information remained more compartmentalized, harder to access by unintended recipients, and was more deniable.[40] Digital remembering, on the other hand, makes much more information accessible to many more recipients for vastly different purposes, while being perceived as undeniably precise and objective.

Stacy's case highlights how the power derived from access to information can lead one to consider self-censorship, a behavior prompted by the accessibility of digital remembering. Andrew Feldmar's case stresses another element. He failed to realize the durability of digital remembering. He got in trouble not because somebody else read his article, but because somebody else read his article years after he had written it. If in hindsight Stacy should have self-censored after considering who, in addition to her friends, might access her web site, Andrew should have constrained his writing based on an unforeseeable future. This makes Andrew's case even more troubling. If we have to imagine how somebody years—perhaps decades into the future—may interpret and weigh our words, we would be even more careful in formulating them. If Stacy's case is part of a *spatial* version of Bentham's panopticon, in which she does not know who watches her but must assume she is watched by everybody, Andrew's story exemplifies an even more constraining *temporal* panopticon.

Will our children be outspoken in online equivalents of school newspapers if they fear their blunt words might hurt their future career? Will we protest against corporate greed or environmental destruction if we worry that these corporations may in some distant future refuse doing business with us? In democracies, individuals are both citizens and consumers. They engage in economic transactions, and take sides on public issues. At times, they may find themselves opposing what their transaction partners advocate. In the analog world, if a person wasn't particularly outspoken, one could easily do both: engage and oppose a transactional partner. Take automobile companies. One can easily buy a car and still advocate for higher emission standards opposed by car manufacturers. Suppose transactional partners knew our views much more precisely. Would they still transact with us, offer us the best price, perhaps even employ us? Just the thought that they might not, may constrain our willingness to act as consumers, let alone as citizens.

Two hundred years after Bentham's original work, French philosopher Michel Foucault argued that the idea of the panopticon has spread in modern times.[41] According to Foucault, not just prisons but other strongly hierarchical organizations like the military, schools, or factories exhibit a pervasive tendency to survey and record. If Foucault were still alive today, he would certainly write about digital remembering as an effective mechanism of panoptic control, both supporting the control in hierarchical organizations and societies, as well as finding support in them, thus cementing and deepening the existing (unequal) distribution of information power.

In short, this has all been about the power associated with information, and its relative nature. As others gain access to our information (especially when we do not approve or even know of it), we lose power and control. Because of the accessibility and durability of digital memory, information power not only shifts from the individual to some known transactional party, but to unknown others as well. This solidifies and deepens existing power differentials between the information rich and the information poor, and may even deny the latter their own conception of their past. Equally problematic, it creates a climate of self-censorship through the perception of panoptic control that constrains robust and open debate—the hallmarks of democratic government—not simply in the present but long into the future.

Time

If my first concern against digital remembering is based on the resulting shifts in control over information and the ensuing loss of individual power, my second argument focuses on how digital remembering negates time, and thereby threatens our ability to decide rationally.

To get a sense of how human decision-making can be influenced by digital remembering, consider the following scenario. One evening at home, Jane receives an e-mail from her friend John. She has known John for two decades but for the last five years or so had seen him only perhaps a dozen times. She still remembers fondly their last meeting, a few months before. They had the type of pleasant wide-ranging conversation only old friends can have. Now John writes that he'll be attending a conference Jane is speaking at and wants to see whether she is free for coffee. Jane is delighted. An idea rushes through her head: why not meet at the little café we found a few years back ... what was its name? Jane searches her mail folder for e-mails she exchanged with John, hoping to come across the café's name. Within a few seconds, dozens of e-mails are displayed, spanning almost a decade, sorted neatly by date, with the oldest on top. She quickly browses through them. As the messages flash by, she recognizes certain words that bring back memories: John's funky car that they would take weekend rides in to the coast, his hideous goatee and how she finally convinced him to get rid of it. Fun times. Then she comes across a very different e-mail of hers; it's short and hurtful, where she accuses her old friend of blatant deception. Jane can't help but read it, then clicks forward. His angry response appears. Then no more e-mails for a year, followed by a trickle of messages that were polite but distant in tone. She goes back to that exchange; the feeling of betrayal in her words, the arrogant denial in his, the deadly e-mail silence leaving her suspended, unsure what exactly had happened, and uncertain how precisely their quarrel played out. But whatever it had been, the idea that John, good old John, blatantly deceived her is suddenly at the forefront of her mind. How could he? And how could she just a few minutes earlier desire to have coffee with him?

Without Jane's wanting to, digital memory revived an event she had failed to recall, muddying her positive emotions towards John. Now she's having difficulties erasing that e-mail exchange from her mind. Jane's reaction is eminently human. That is how human memory works. Over time, and helped by subsequent pleasant experiences, Jane's memory of John had become overwhelmingly positive. Searching her digital memory for a piece of information—the name of the café—confronted her with the angry e-mail exchange years ago. Her analytic mind wants to disregard the old quarrel. Let bygones be bygones. Her conflict with John happened years before, and even though John behaved irresponsibly, she had apparently forgiven him to the point that she had even forgotten the conflict. But the angry words she read triggered her memory. They are the external stimuli that help us reactivate the links to memories we thought lost. Slowly, a few—and unpleasant—elements of that fight with John return to her. Once more, she brushes them aside, and decides to meet with John. But will she be able to greet him in a fresh frame of mind, without a trace of anger? Just an hour earlier, she would have said emphatically yes. Now she's no longer certain.

The story of Jane and John is fictional, but the processes I describe are deeply rooted in human behavior, with how we remember and how we sense our own past. Two peculiarities of the way humans remember complicate the picture. The first has to do with how memory fades. We all know that we remember less clearly what happened further in the past than what happened more recently. But that's only a crude rule of thumb. Closer to the truth is that we remember best what we remember often. The very act of remembering makes it more likely that we'll be able to retrieve that piece of memory in the future.

What we recall less frequently, on the other hand, fades more quickly, to the point where we have difficulty recalling it at all. In a related fashion, we have a better recall of memories that resonate with the context we are currently in. If we are happy, we will recall happy memories; if we are depressed, it is more difficult for us to remember good times. In addition, we remember more easily what confirms our current beliefs, rather than what contradicts them. We may still be able to retrieve nonconforming events that we were initially unable to recall, but it may require a comprehensive or sustained stimulus—as with Jane reading old e-mails between her and John. Together, this points towards inherent limitations in how humans comprehend their past—and if we are confronted with a tension between cues provided by digital memory and our immediate human recollection, we are struggling to put these different pieces of remembering in perspective.

The second idiosyncrasy of how we remember is that our brain does not treat all types of retrieval cues alike. From 1978 to 1984, Dutch psychologist Willem Wagenaar kept a detailed diary of his life.[42] Every day he recorded the most important event of that day, where it happened and who was with him, but during these years of recordkeeping he never allowed himself to look at the diary entries he'd earlier written—he did not want them to trigger any internal memories. Afterwards, he tried to randomly remember recorded events using partial cues from his diary. For example, he read what had happened on a particular day, and then tried to remember where it happened, who was with him when it happened, and what the exact date of the event was. Expectedly, cues helped him greatly in recalling events which otherwise he would have had much greater difficulty remembering. But, unexpectedly, cues did not work equally well. By a significant margin, using "what" to remember "who," "where," and "when" worked best, followed by a fairly equally effective "where" and "who" cue. In contrast, the "when" cue failed to work in almost all cases—knowing a specific date almost never helped Wagenaar remember the important event of that day. Wagenaar's results reflect the great difficulty humans have in sorting and retrieving memory based on the passing of time.

Of course, a precise date (like April 30, 1971) is perhaps too artificial a time mark for people to associate events with. Since pinpointing a specific date is hard, Wagenaar thought that perhaps recalling events using relative time might be easier. To find out, for a couple of hundred days he noted not one daily event but two in his diary, and marked these days. He hoped that he could use one event as the cue for the other—if our memory is not sorted sequentially, perhaps events we remember have at least relative links to events immediately before or after. They don't, as he discovered. Humans do not only have great difficulties remembering events based on exact time cues, but likely also on relative time cues. Time is quite simply a very difficult dimension of memory for humans to master.[43] We are all familiar with that. People frequently talk about putting events "into perspective"—not because this is easy (we would not talk about it if it were), but because it is hard.

Why exactly we, like Jane, have difficulties sequencing events with the perspective of time in mind is not yet clear. One possible key to understanding this seeming deficiency of ours is human forgetting. By letting our memory of past events fade over time, we already have in place a perfectly functioning mechanism that puts these in a temporal perspective. Because biological forgetting is built into our human physiology, through the millennia of human evolution we never had to develop an alternative cognitive ability to correctly valuate events in our past. Such an explanation fits with how evolution generally works, as a pragmatic and conservative process. Preference is given to the tried and tested method, the one that already works, rather than a more complex (and thus potentially error-prone) alternative. In our case, this may have left us with biological forgetting, rather than the ability for a detailed cognitive understanding of time past.

As we undermine biological forgetting through the use of digital memory, we make ourselves vulnerable to indecision or incorrect judgment, just like Jane. This is the curse of digital re-membering. It goes much beyond the confines of shifts in information power, and to the heart of our ability as humans to *act in time.*

In Borges' short story, Funes cannot help remembering every detail of every moment of his life.[44] Incapable of forgetting, Funes remains forever caught in his memories, unable to think. "To think," Borges writes, "is to ignore (or forget) differences, to generalize, to abstract. Since his accident, Funes is condemned to only see the trees, and never the forest. In the teeming world of Ireneo Funes there was nothing but particulars."[45] Perfect remembering for Borges threatens to afflict its victim with a never-receding cacophony of information from which no clear abstract thought emerges, that thus imprisons those afflicted much like Marcel Proust in his *In Search of Lost Time*[46]—whereas human forgetting is the very quality that lets us rise above the particular to grasp the general.

Without our ability to forget, whenever faced with a decision we would always recall all our past decisions, resulting in potential indecision, much as how AJ, the woman with near perfect memory, describes it. "I remember good, which is very comforting," AJ says. "But I also remember bad—and every bad choice. And I really don't give myself a break. There are all these forks in the road, moments you have to make a choice, and then it's ten years later, and I'm still beating myself up over them. I don't forgive myself for a lot of things. Your memory is the way it is to protect you. I feel like it just hasn't protected me. [. . .] Most people have called what I have a gift, but I call it a burden."[47] And later, in her recently published autobiography, AJ writes "Though people tend to think of forgetting as an affliction and are disturbed by the loss of so much memory as they age, I've come to understand that there is a real value to being able to forget a good deal about our lives."[48]

Seen this way, forgetting is not an annoying flaw but a life-saving advantage. As we forget, we regain the freedom to generalize, conceptualize, and most importantly to act. Take Jane, before reading her old e-mails, she saw John as a friend. Her mind had forgotten the old conflict, precisely because it was no longer important, because the value of its memory was superseded by later and contradicting events. A relatively crude mechanism, biological forgetting led Jane to assume that John and she were friends. Digital memory, on the other hand, had brought back forgotten information, causing Jane to become conflicted in her judgment, lose decisiveness, and be in danger of perhaps choosing inaccurately. Moreover, forgetting may be instrumental for the process of learning. As organizational learning expert William Starbuck writes, learning something completely new requires that one first "unlearns" the old and obsolete.[49] Biological forgetting is a tremendously simple and elegant way of such unlearning. In contrast, digital memory may keep our remembering of existing knowledge so current that our ability to learn is inhibited.[50]

Thus, as we expand the use of external memory through digital remembering, we endanger human reasoning a number of ways. Three of them I have already mentioned. First, external memory may act as a memory cue, causing us to recall events we thought we had forgotten. If human forgetting is at least in part a constructive process of filtering information based on relevance, a recall triggered by digital memory of an event that our brain has "forgotten" may undermine human reasoning. Second, comprehensive digital memory may exacerbate the human difficulty of putting past events in proper temporal sequence. Third, digital remembering may confront us with too much of our past and thus impede our ability to decide and act in time (similar to what AJ and Funes experienced), as well as to learn.

The fourth danger is that when confronted with digital memory that conflicts with our human recollection of events, we may lose trust in our own remembering. As outlined in chapter 2, humans remember remarkably well, but our memory does not leave stored information untouched. Recall is not like taking a book off a library shelf, which after dusting it off a bit, contains the exact same information as at the time we put it there. Recall is retrieving from a corpus of memories that is ever changing, and which is reconstructed by our mind to take into account subsequent experiences, preferences, and biases. Despite having been rewritten many times, humans trust their memories, and thus trust in the past they remember. At times, this leads to disconcerting situations in which two people have two very different recollections of a past event. We find such situations annoying, and our brain helps us overcome them by tending to focus on the parts our memories have in common, rather than those that differ. Such divergences of the past we remember will happen much more frequently and bluntly when we are confronted with digital memory that deviates from our own recollection. Who should we trust in such a situation—our mind or the external memory? Logic tells us the latter, although our intuition tempts us to believe in ourselves. As digital remembering relentlessly exposes discrepancies between factual bits and our very own human recall, what we may lose in the process is the trust in the past *as we remember it.*

Of course, this may not necessarily be all bad. As I have suggested, human memory is not perfect; frequently it fails us. In such situations digital memory may be beneficial, since we may force ourselves when memory discrepancies arise to trust digital memory rather than our own. Trusting the past as we remember it would be replaced by trusting the past as it is reflected in digital memory. While requiring great discipline, it offers the advantage of converging memory—that the past we trust in is the same others trust as well. But trusting digital memory more than our own human recollection exposes us to yet another challenge: what if external memory itself (digital memory in particular) is not unalterable, but can be modified after the fact, and thus does not necessarily represent an accurate rendition of a past event? If we all trust the same source, we are all equally vulnerable to its alterability.

Exercising control over a society's past is a hallmark of dictatorial regimes—even if that entails forging public documents. For example, in the Soviet Union, graphic artists were tasked with retouching disgraced comrades out of public photographs, thereby erasing evidence of their presence—even their existence—from shared external memory.[51] Written more than half a century ago, George Orwell's *1984* lays out in eloquent and shocking detail what happens to a society in which the past is no longer controlled by each individual, but made malleable by the central authorities of the ruling regime. In such a society, Orwell explains, "[h]istory is continuously rewritten. This day-to-day falsification of the past, carried out by the Ministry of Truth, is as necessary to the stability of the regime as the work of repression and espionage carried out by the Ministry of Love. [...] The past is whatever the records and the memories agree upon. And since the Party is in full control of all records and in equally full control of the minds of its members, it follows that the past is whatever the Party chooses to make it. It also follows that though the past is alter-able, it never has been altered in any specific instance. For when it has been recreated in whatever shape is needed at the moment, then this new version *is* the past, and no different past can ever have existed."[52] If we replace the trust in our past with the trust in digital memory, dictatorial regimes will no longer have to control our minds. Controlling the externalized mem-ory of our collective past will suffice. And Orwell's dystopian vision may become much more likely.

Altering external memories no longer requires sophisticated graphic artists as in the Soviet Union, or eloquent censors as in Orwell's *1984*. Wikipedia, the impressive online encyclopedia hundreds of millions use frequently, can be altered by anybody who so desires.[53] Many errors are quickly spotted, but by far not all of them—as a growing list of cases demonstrates.[54] With widely available digital photo software like Adobe Photoshop Elements, even the most casual users can alter a digital image to make faces smile when they did not, or to retouch dimples and wrinkles. In fact, a small cottage industry of services now exists that offers to retouch ex-spouses out of holiday photos and group shots. Thus, in the world of digital memory, no lon-ger is it only Big Brother that can alter the past—it is everyone.

To be sure, forgeries are no invention of the digital age. They have been with us for thousands of years—from the Donation of Constantine (a forged Roman edict from the eighth century) to Michelangelo's Cupid (a sculpture he deliberately made look antique) to Hitler's diaries.[55] And herein lies the first difference: because we are familiar with faked analog memory, we ap-proach it cautiously, examine it carefully, and allocate our trust in it accordingly. Digital memory we find more believable, in part precisely because the skills we learned evaluating analog memory—inspecting the surface of a document, and whether it has been tampered with, for example—fail to reveal digital forgeries. Perhaps over time we'll adjust, and approach digital memory with the appropriate level of caution and the skills to reveal falsifications. In the interim, however, the superficial authenticity of digital memory may only confuse us further.[56]

The second difference is posed by the seeming comprehensiveness of digital memory. In the analog world, we understand that a piece of external memory—a handwritten note, a photo, a document—is only one element to comprehend a past event. To grasp an event as fully as possible, we accept that we have to search very different sources in a number of different ways, and our queries will result in mismatched puzzle pieces failing to fit together perfectly. Similar to how we remember, we don't simply recall an event but *reconstruct* it. To do it well requires a lot of time and effort, as historians can attest. This is fundamentally different for digital memory, where following our query a full plate of information pieces about a past event appears within seconds. Awed by the speed and comprehensiveness of the results, we assume that what we have been presented with is, in fact, a complete set of puzzle pieces, and all we have to do is put it back together. It is similar to how some of my students respond when I tell them their research is incomplete: "But that was all I could find through Google!"

What digital remembering yields is not the entire picture, but at best only those elements of it that are captured in digital memory. What if—to use our scenario—Jane and John had a long, emotional, and honest face-to-face conversation about their quarrel? What if at the end of that they embraced and set out to rebuild their friendship? That would be a fundamentally important piece for Jane in assessing John's action. Yet, if it happened "in person" rather than over e-mail, Jane's digital memory will not retrieve it. Reconstructing the past without that important piece results in a fundamentally incomplete picture. Of course, the information we have to ground our decisions in is almost always incomplete—by necessity. But in the analog world, random pieces of information are missing. With digital memory, the exclusion is biased against information that is not captured in digital form and not fed into digital memory. That is a systematic bias, and one that not only falsifies our understanding of events but that can also be gamed. In short, because digital memory amplifies only digitized information, humans like Jane trusting digital memory may find themselves worse off than if they'd relied solely on their human memory, with its tendency to forget information that is no longer important or relevant.

I began by suggesting that digital remembering negates time. By triggering recall of what we thought we had long forgotten, digital remembering has the ability to confuse us with conflicting memories that may cloud our judgment. We may decide incorrectly, or waver and thus fail to act. We may stop trusting our own memory, and thus our own past, supplanting it not with an objective past but an artificial one. It's a past that is neither ours nor anybody else's; instead it is a synthetic past reconstructed from the limited information digital memory has stored about it, an utterly skewed patchwork devoid of time and open to manipulation in both what it contains, and what it doesn't. I fear that by denying ourselves our own past, we may damage our ability to judge—and more so than we think.

But there is one further dimension of how digital remembering negates time. Earlier I mentioned digital dossiers and results of person queries in search engines. They are odd because they are limited to information available in digital format, and thus omit (possibly important) facts not stored in digital memory. Equally odd is how in such dossiers time is collapsed, and years—perhaps decades of life—are thrown together: that a person took out a loan a decade ago may be found next to the link to an academic paper she published six years later, as well as a picture posted on Flickr only last week. The resulting collage with all the missing (as well as possibly misleading) bits is no accurate reflection of the person themselves. Using an ever more comprehensive set of digital sources does not help much either. The resulting digital collage of facts would still be problematic. It would be like taking a box of unsorted photos of yourself, throwing them on a table and thinking that by just looking hard enough at them you might gain a comprehensive accurate sense of who the person in the photos actually is *today* (if you think this example is far-fetched, just look at Flickr, and how it makes accessible photos taken over long periods of time). These digital collages combine innumerous bits of information about us, each one (at best) having been valid at a certain point in our past. But as it is presented to us, it is information from which time has been eliminated; a collage in which change is visible only as tension between two contradicting facts, not as an evolutionary process, taking place over time.

Some worry that digital collages resemble momentary comprehensive snapshots of us frozen in time, like a photograph, but accessible to the world. Actually, digital collages are much more disquieting than that. They are not like one, but hundreds, perhaps thousands of snapshots taken over our lifetime superimposed over each other, but without the perspective of time. How can we grasp a sense of a person that way? How can we hope to understand how a person evolved over the years, adjusting his views, adapting to his (changing) environment? How can we pretend to know who that person is today, and how his values, his thinking, his character have evolved, when all that we are shown is a timeless collage of personal facts thrown together? Perhaps, the advocates of digital memory would retort that we could do so with appropriate digital filters, where through visual presentation time could be reintroduced, like color-coding years, or sorting events. I am afraid it still might not fully address the problem. Because I fear the real bottleneck of conflating history and collapsing time is not digital memory, but human comprehension. Even if we were presented with a dossier of facts, neatly sorted by date, in our mind we would still have difficulties putting things in the right temporal perspective, valuing facts properly over time. That is the quintessence of Jane's dilemma. From the perspective of the person remembering, digital memory impedes judgment. From the perspective of the person remembered, however, it denies development, and refuses to acknowledge that all humans change all the time. By recalling forever each of our errors and transgressions, digital memory rejects our human capacity to learn from them, to grow and to evolve.

If human actions are never forgotten, there is little need for people to push themselves and change. In a world of omnipresent history, there may be little incentive to actively work on escaping one's caste and breaking out of one's mold, a fundamental element of modern enlightened society. Of course, even without incentives, humans as living beings will continue to change in a digital world—we'll age physically and modify our views—but our digital representations will forever tether us to all our past actions, making it impossible, in practice, to escape them. Without some form of forgetting, forgiving becomes a difficult undertaking. Or as T. S. Eliot wrote, "[i]f all time is eternally present, [a]ll time is unredeemable."[57]

Memory impedes change. That is true for all memory. In analog times, however, memory remained expensive—and comprehensive, timely, and affordable access to it was largely illusive. We used external memory deliberately, not casually, and not all the time. Employed sparingly and judiciously, memory is a valuable treasure, it seasons our decision-making like a delicate spice. Digital remembering, on the other hand, today is so omnipresent, costless, and seemingly "valuable"—due to accessibility, durability, and comprehensiveness—that we are tempted to employ it constantly. Utilized in such indiscriminating fashion, digital memory not only dulls the judgment of the ones who remember but also denies those who are remembered the temporal space to evolve.

There is one final wrinkle regarding time. As I have suggested, digital remembering may prompt us to cease trusting our human memory, preferring digital memory instead. This way, digital memory is elevated to the primary source of reconstructing the past: easy to use and comprehensive, as well as seemingly more accurate and objective than the fallible memory of the forgetful human mind. But more so than atoms, information bits are malleable—as I mentioned, they can easily be changed, and thus history altered. What happens when people realize that the past can no longer be trusted? Perhaps the answer to this question may be similar to the one asking how people will live with digital memory that never forgets, thereby denying change. If our past—constructed from digital memory—is no longer trustworthy, and no longer useful, we might disregard it. In the best of worlds, this leads us back to human forgetting (and human remembering), perhaps with an infrequent but valuable use of digital memory—and this I would cheer. But things might not turn out that well. We may enter a time in which—as a reaction to too much remembering, with too strict and unforgiving a link to our past—some may opt for the extreme and ignore the past altogether for the present, deciding to live just in the moment.

This may sound more far-fetched than it actually is. Take the culture of short messaging (SMSing). Most of the messages sent back and forth (much like one's status on Facebook) are, as Internet entrepreneur Joi Ito reminded me, not intended to communicate something about the past or the future, but are solely about the present: this is where I am; this is what I do. These messages are intentionally ephemeral, capturing the fleeting moment that is now, nothing beyond. At least to some extent this may be how the digital generation responds to digital remembering. But this overemphasis on the now and here may be throwing out the baby with the bathwater, in an understandable but unhealthy oscillation towards the other extreme—from an all-pervading past to an utterly ignorant present. Neither of these extremes is useful. Instead, we need to realize that human existence has the capacity to both remember *and* forget.

In this chapter, I have laid out the predicaments we face as we fail to forget. Under the rubric of power, I described how digital memory deepens the already existing chasm between the information rich and the information poor, further empowering the former to the detriment of the latter. I explained how comprehensive digital memory stifles societal debate. At the interface of power and time, permanent remembering creates the specter of a spatial and temporal panopticon, in which everybody may constantly be tempted to self-censor. Perhaps most importantly, comprehensive digital remembering collapses history, impairing our judgment and our capacity to act in time. It denies us humans the chance to evolve, develop, and learn, leaving us helplessly oscillating between two equally troubling options: a permanent past and an ignorant present.

CHAPTER V

Potential Responses

If digital remembering may cause such profound consequences, how are we to react? In this chapter, I detail six possible responses aimed at preventing or mitigating the challenges of power and time posed by digital memory. The six responses differ, not just in substance but also to the extent we know whether they work or not. Two of them have been implemented in quite a number of societies. For them, we have relatively good (if qualitative) data on their effectiveness. The remaining ones have been proposed, but they have not been widely used. Therefore, my evaluation of them will have to be more speculative.

Digital Abstinence

This approach rests on the view that individuals play a central role in responding to digital remembering. The fundamental idea is that once people understand the implications of abandoning forgetting, they will stop providing their personal information to others, and digital memory will cease to exist—at least in the comprehensive and threatening form I described. After all, if Stacy had not put her photo on her MySpace web page for the world to see, she would not have gotten into trouble, and if Andrew Feldmar had not submitted his manuscript to a journal that later was also available online, he would still be able to travel freely into the United States. If one abstains from putting personal information online, one does not have to fear the consequences of an enduring digital memory—neither loss of control and power over information, nor being exposed to the digital panopticon or impaired reasoning.

The solution seems simple and straightforward: stay away as much as possible from interactions that force you to reveal information to others. To achieve such behavioral change, individuals will need to be educated to understand how much information they routinely provide to others, the value of that information, and the dangers associated with storing and repurposing that information with the help of digital memory. The digital abstinence approach assumes that people will adjust their behavior once the potential abuse of personal information has become apparent to them. That knowledge will spread the seed of change and lead to a mass movement of people abstaining from feeding their personal information into digital memory, which in turn cripples digital remembering and restores a forgetting society. Digital abstinence has a certain Luddite ring to it, a view that opposes technological progress. But unlike some hardcore neo-Luddites that want us to forego the use of technology altogether, digital abstinence is singularly focused on limiting uncontrollable information flows through individual choice.[1]

Digital abstinence, based on an individual's knowledge and preferences, does not depend on the passage of regulatory measures and their enforcement, but rests on individuals' decisions, on norms individuals have themselves chosen to follow rather than laws or other external constraints that have been forced upon them.

The success of such an approach depends on a number of factors. The first is that it works by influencing people's behavior. This requires educating people on how damaging the misuse of their personal information can be, and what can be done to avoid it. That is a tall order. Over the past years, the media have repeatedly reported on the potential negative consequences of information privacy invasions, but we have yet to witness a sea change in public attitudes. In fact, as Harvard Berkman Center's John Palfrey and Urs Gasser write, young digital natives around the world are less discriminate and more trusting in sharing personal information with others.[2] Digital abstinence, or even the realization of the dangers they face in a world of digital memory clearly is not widespread. Of course, this may change. As reports of negative effects of digital memory become more common, and knowledge of cases like Stacy Snyder's and Andrew Feldmar's spreads, more people may take notice. One of the surprising, and heartening consequences (at least for me) of my initial paper on the virtue of forgetting in the digital age has been the strong and sustained public interest in learning about the potential dangers of digital remembering. If that is any indication, perhaps taking that first hurdle of educating users about what they can do to limit their personal exposure may not be infeasible after all.

Getting people to understand digital memory and its implications, however, is only the first step. It will prove useless if it is not followed by a change in actual behavior. For digital abstinence to work, people must resist posting personal information online. They also must select transactional partners, including ecommerce sites like Amazon or search engines like Google, based on how little personal information these partners require.

The problem is that sharing personal information offers users value, which individuals may not want to forego. In exchange for receiving personal information, ecommerce vendors provide their customers with customized (and thus more valuable) transactional experiences: Amazon offers book recommendations, and Google serves up more targeted lists of search results. Are individuals willing to give up these benefits *en masse* to combat the dangers of digital memory? This is not just about quality, efficiency, and economic benefits. An entire generation of users has grown up utilizing the Internet not just as a network to access information, but to share information with others. Over one hundred million people have a MySpace page, just like Stacy Snyder. And two out of three young Americans have shared content with the rest of the world on the Internet, just like Andrew. The majority of younger Internet users enjoy living in a world of thick information ties, in which they can share their thoughts and experiences with others, expand opportunities, and carry out transactions efficiently. It is unlikely they are willing to forego all of that and pledge digital abstinence, except if sharing their information exposes them to some real, substantial threat.[3] This is a difficult danger to prove, at least in the short term. Negative consequences of digital remembering will rarely impact us now; they will instead return to haunt us in future years. Persuading people to forego a concrete present benefit in order to avoid potential future troubles is a hard sell.

Maybe that is a good thing. As Harvard Law professor Yochai Benkler has argued so persuasively, the participation of millions of Internet users around the world in creating content has unleashed innovative and beneficial forms of information production that would not have been possible in a world of digital abstinence.[4] Plus, John Seely Brown's digital bricolages—offering powerful combinations and recombinations of information to produce creative works (also mentioned in chapter 3)—would be much harder to build. If such steps mean giving up the social innovations of production and sharing that Yochai Benkler and John Seely Brown talk about, perhaps the idea of digital abstinence itself is too radical, too binary, forcing us to become digital recluses and forego many of the valuable benefits of the digital age.

Maybe the core idea of digital abstinence—that humans ought to be more careful when contributing information online—can be useful if it is stripped of its extremeness. One could envision, for example, "digital abstinence light." Instead of expecting individuals to keep most information to themselves, people would just be expected to be more cautious when releasing information. Such an approach would accept that in many circumstances providing information to others creates value, not just for the group but also for oneself. By the same token, digital abstinence light would still aim to educate and empower people to choose carefully before sharing their personal information with others. Since information processors—from ecommerce vendors to providers of information-sharing platforms—could no longer assume that individuals share their personal information with them, they would have to adjust their business practices and accept substantial limitations to digital remembering.[5]

Such a "light" approach overcomes the radical absoluteness inherent in the original idea of digital abstinence. Its effectiveness depends on the pressure individuals can and will exert on information vendors. Unlike with digital abstinence and its clear-cut rule to refuse sharing personal information, unfortunately the very advantage of digital abstinence light—its reliance on flexibility and individual judgment—is also its likely Achilles heel, for at least two reasons. The first is that individuals are left to their devices when negotiating with information-processing vendors whether to release information. Given the power imbalance between the two sides, such negotiations structurally disadvantage the individual. Information processors can easily aggregate information about individuals' digital abstinence preferences to shape negotiations and a user's decision-making (for example, through clever messaging). In contrast, the individual has to decide without knowing how others have decided, and whether and how competitors of their negotiation counterpart might respond. Because of the inherent information power differential, individuals will have a difficult time insisting on a light form of digital abstinence. Second (and related), individuals are caught in a dilemma. For each one of them it would be beneficial if all others refused to provide personal information for a given service, so that through pressure vendors would adjust their information collection and storage behavior. By the same token, individually and in the short run each one of them gains from providing personal information to a vendor, for example, because they'll receive a particular service. The result might be a version of preaching water but drinking wine: widespread public rhetoric for digital abstinence, paired with private mass defections to enjoy the benefits of information sharing.[6]

The inability and unwillingness of individuals to give up information sharing is undermining the effectiveness of digital abstinence in its "light" version to counter digital remembering. But even if people were to alter their behavior and share their personal information much more cautiously and selectively, the effectiveness of digital abstinence would still be in doubt. Information is hard to trace and contain. Once I have passed on information to somebody else, I need to trust that person to keep my information confidential, but I have no direct control over it anymore. Therefore, even if one provides personal information only to a handful of selected transactional partners, there is no guarantee that the recipient of the personal information will use it as promised. And when such information is passed on from one vendor to another, it is difficult if not impossible to find out who violated one's trust and leaked the information to whom. No form of digital abstinence addresses such leakage, because the concept of abstinence is solely focused on the individual's decision to release information, and does not take into account subsequent decisions by vendors of whether to share that information with third parties. Finally, even if we became digitally abstinent tomorrow, the vast amounts of personal information already available would continue to render us vulnerable for decades to come. Why would we want to stop giving away our personal information if it is already out there anyway, and shared among others?

At first digital abstinence seemed an intriguing concept, until we realized that getting people to constrain what they desire to share is difficult. Expecting a good fit between stopping digital remembering and selective disclosure, we are reminded that personal information once released is very difficult to contain. Even if individuals adjust their information sharing behavior, information processors may have little incentive to follow suit.

This weakness in enforcement can be addressed by employing laws rather than social norms, as well as market incentives that individuals may or may not follow. This is the domain of information privacy rights.

Information Privacy Rights

A viable and accepted mechanism of enforcement is a defining quality of information privacy rights. Such rights come in vastly different forms and shapes, but at the core they share the same principle: providing individuals with a legally recognized claim over their personal information, thereby empowering them to maintain informational control. As such, information privacy rights seem a suitable response to the troubling erosion of information power and control caused by digital memory. In its most basic form, information privacy rights give individuals a right to choose whether or not to share information. If somebody obtains personal information by snooping on others without their consent, she would violate the law and be subject to punishment.

The first famous advocates of such privacy rights were Boston attorneys Samuel Warren and Louis Brandeis (later Supreme Court Justice Brandeis), who in 1890 published their article "The Right to Privacy" in the *Harvard Law Review*, advocating essentially for the recognition of a tort to address invasions of privacy.[7] They took on the subject, it is said, after unkindly reports appeared in the local press on Warren's dinner parties.[8] This helps explain the limited threat they desired to address: privacy intrusions, or in the parlance of the information age, using personal information without an individual's consent.

It also reveals a fundamental challenge information privacy rights face. Whether or not they are effective in protecting an individual's control over her personal information depends on how exactly such a right is being structured. I may consent for the Post Office to have my new address, but not for the Post Office to pass it on to third parties. How can I stop this from happening? If I were given a simple property right in my personal information, by transferring property to an information processor I would relinquish any control over that information. That's not what is needed. Therefore, information privacy rights require a carefully crafted legal mechanism to work, especially since in practice it will be enormously difficult for individuals to identify the source of an information leak, and thus the appropriate party to sue. Think, for example, of the information that an individual takes anti-depressants. That information could have been leaked by the doctor, the pharmacist, the insurance company, any employee of these, even a friend, spouse, or colleague who knows. It's often next to impossible to identify the culprit and thus to get effective enforcement. That is why many jurisdictions around the world conceptualize information privacy rights as binding all subsequent users of an individual's personal information, not just the one that an individual has entrusted with it.

The danger that one will lose control over information, however, is not only manifest when a lawful recipient of personal information passes it on to a third party without the individual's consent. The danger is also present when an individual has given somebody her personal information for a particular purpose, and then the information is subsequently used for a different purpose. For example, if a bank collects and stores personal information from a customer for the express purpose of assessing whether the customer is eligible for a loan, customers may not like that the bank reuses that information for direct marketing purposes on credit cards without their express consent. That is why more sophisticated information privacy rights come with a purpose limitation principle—a legal constraint that the recipient of personal information can only use that information for the purposes to which you consented, and no others.

Information privacy rights also differ widely in scope. In the United States, the federal Privacy Act of 1974 only covers processing of personal information by federal agencies.[9] Americans have no federally codified general right to information privacy vis-à-vis any body outside the federal government.[10] In Europe, legislatures were bolder (perhaps due to the long shadow cast by Europe's violent and brutal twentieth-century history), and so empowered individuals with information privacy rights not just vis-à-vis the central government, but all public and private sector information processors. Moreover, beginning with Germany in the mid-1980s,[11] the Europeans moved towards a much broader concept of information privacy rights, leaving behind the Warren/Brandeis right to privacy.[12] If the original information privacy rights were more focused on the question of individual consent, information privacy is now seen as an individual's right to shape her participation in society.[13] In an interconnected world, the right to information privacy can no longer be understood as a binary right of consent, of an absolute yes or no, but has to be reconstituted in a much more nuanced fashion, linking consent with the specific purposes and conditions of information processing. It is a right to determine primarily *how*—rather than *whether*—one participates in sharing information. This broader conception, often called the right to informational self-determination is intended to give individuals control over every phase and stage of the use of their personal information.

It is a sophisticated yet complex setup. When information privacy rights gave individuals just a simple choice whether or not to consent to the processing of their personal information, enforcement was comparatively simple. Information processors had to demonstrate that each individual consented. With a broader concept of informational self-determination, individuals consent based on a particular purpose and context of information processing. This necessitates that information processors keep track not only of who consented but also for what purpose. This applies to instances where individuals are compelled by law to provide information as well (think of providing your driver's license to a police officer when you have been stopped for speeding, or handing over your financial information to a court as part of bankruptcy proceedings).

The result is a powerful combination of broad information privacy rights with purpose limitation rules. This has two advantages over digital abstinence. First, individuals now have the means—the legal system—to enforce their control rights over information. Second, purpose limitation rules ensure that information is not being reused and shared except with individual consent. Unfortunately, such legal privacy protection mechanisms also comes with three substantial drawbacks: they are notoriously difficult to enact, at least in the United States; they are shockingly underutilized, at least in Europe; and they depend on our society's willingness to abide by present information privacy principles in the future.

Empowering individuals to control their personal information entails constraining the information collection, storage, processing, and distribution of others, who may think that their activity is protected by a fundamental right, like the freedom of speech, or at the very least is part of the basic economic freedom central to market economies. The resulting tension has made comprehensive information privacy legislation beyond the public sector and some narrow confines of private sector use politically infeasible in the United States, at least so far. At times in the past three decades, more comprehensive information privacy legislation has been debated in Congress, but no mass movement developed. Political scientists may have a general explanation why. Legislation often is enacted, they suggest, when it is favored by a clearly defined, highly motivated, and well-funded group, and when most citizens stand to lose too little to fight.[14] Comprehensive information privacy legislation is the exact opposite: most citizens perceive to gain a little (but too little to be motivated to act), while the motivated and well-funded group of information processors fear they will lose a lot. Of course, given the potentially grave consequences (and high losses), eventually digital remembering may trigger enough of a mass movement to demand information privacy for Congress to be pushed to enact a comprehensive information privacy law. However, given the political dynamic of past decades, I would not bet on it.

Politics is one reason no federal statute has passed in the United States empowering individuals with a broad range of information privacy rights. Another may be substantial doubts about its effectiveness. European nations have decades of experience granting individuals rights to ensure information privacy, with Germany among the top. In the early 1990s, I asked all Germany data protection commissioners to send me cases of individuals who had used information privacy rights to hold information processors financially liable for collecting, storing, or processing personal information without consent. The surprising response was that they knew of none—not a single case! Granted, they may not know of all cases, but still the result is puzzling. One possible explanation why individuals simply failed to enforce their information privacy rights in court may be that legal enforcement is generally risky, and takes time and effort. Moreover, to enforce their claims to informational privacy in court, individuals have to shed their anonymity, which many may not want to do. There may also be too little to be gained since German liability law only permits actual damages to be awarded (which are notoriously difficult to calculate in information privacy cases).

Perhaps then information privacy rights need to be bolstered with changes in the legal procedures necessary to enforce them. Possible measures could include shifting the burden of proof from the individual to the information processor, letting criminal rather than civil courts take on enforcement, or lowering court costs to encourage individuals to litigate their information privacy claims. Convinced that this would make a difference, European legislatures revised their information privacy statutes to incorporate a number of these measures.[15] More than a decade has passed since these revisions and my informal queries around European information privacy agencies reveal that relatively little has changed; cases of individuals suing information processors remain rare. Of course, information processors could have complied so comprehensively with individual's information privacy rights that no legal enforcement had been necessary; or perhaps enforcement action had taken place outside of the narrow confines of civil liability claims. It may also be that measures taken are badly implemented or insufficiently communicated to the public. Still, the persistence of these results must trouble proponents of information privacy rights on both sides of the Atlantic: individuals (at least in Europe) seem to be reluctant to dedicate enough time and effort to enforce their information privacy rights.

Information privacy rights are saddled with a third inherent drawback, one associated with trust. Trust is necessary because as individuals share their personal information with others, they lose direct control over it. Individuals can trust information processors that they won't misuse personal information. This is the concept of digital abstinence. Or they can trust a societal institution—the law—to bring about compliance (as with information privacy rights). The advantage of information privacy rights is that individuals retain some legal control over their personal information even after they have shared it with others. But for such control to endure, enforcement must be ensured not just in the present, but also in the future. What is my information privacy right good for, if a year from now information privacy rights are abolished, and information processors sitting on huge piles of personal information can use it as they see fit? Consequently some nations have afforded information privacy rights constitutional guarantees, making it harder to abolish them in the future. But outright abolition might not be necessary to undermine the effectiveness of information privacy rights since these rights depend on the readiness of governments to enforce them. When government no longer believes in privacy, it will not vigorously enforce it, rendering individuals vulnerable.

This may sound abstract and unlikely, but the twentieth century provides a gripping case. In the 1930s, the Dutch government had put in place a comprehensive population registry containing name, birth date, address, religion, and other personal information for each citizen.[16] The registry was hailed as facilitating government administration and improving welfare planning. Then the Nazis invaded the Netherlands and took possession of the registry, ruthlessly repurposing the personal information of millions of Dutch citizens to identify, persecute, and murder Jews and gypsies. Because of the information contained in the comprehensive registry, the Nazis were able to identify, deport, and murder a much higher percentage (73 percent) of the Dutch Jewish population than in Belgium (40 percent), France (25 percent), or any other European nation. Even Jewish refugees in the Netherlands fared better than Dutch Jews because the refugees (in contrast to Jewish citizens) could avoid being included in the registry. Gypsies, the other population group the Nazis persecuted with the help of the population registry, fared even worse. The lesson is obvious: The Dutch provided their personal information trusting their government, and not anticipating the Nazi invasion. We may feel safe living in democratic republics, but so did the Dutch. We do not know what the future holds in store for us, and whether future governments will honor the trust we put in them to protect information privacy rights.

Difficult to enact, of dubious effectiveness, and with no insurance against an uncertain future, the overall suitability of information privacy rights to counter digital remembering is unclear.

Maybe the problem is that we have misconceived information privacy rights and slotted them incorrectly into existing but unsuitable legal categories like torts, or novel but overly complex rights, like the one on informational self-determination. Perhaps alternative conceptions of information privacy rights would be more effective in protecting us from the threat posed by comprehensive digital memory. Berkeley law professor Pamela Samuelson has suggested that a contractual approach, using elements of trade secrecy laws, may be more fruitful.[17] This could lead, she argues, to default licensing rules of personal information, thus ensuring individuals retain their control (and power) over their information. It has the advantage of flexibility over more rigid regimes of information privacy rights, and is based on accepted mechanisms rather than relying on complex new legal tools. Rather than focusing on the most appropriate legal mechanism to implement information privacy rights, New York University professor Helen Nissenbaum has proposed to focus on the context in which information gathering and dissemination takes place.[18] For her, the task of rights protecting individuals' information power is to ensure that information is not disconnected from its context. Nissenbaum's idea is a corollary to the purpose limitation principle, but rather than looking at the purpose of information use, her aim is to take into account the context in which that use takes place. This prevents the decontextualization of information I described in earlier chapters, even in cases when the overall purpose of information use stays constant. Another approach has been suggested by George Washington University law professor Daniel Solove, who argues for information privacy rights that are focused on the reputational dimension of information. It implies that the danger is not the loss of control over one's information, but the tarnishing of one's reputation through such information.[19] While traditional information privacy rights as well as Samuelson's and Nissenbaum's proposals concentrate more on how (and under what conditions) information flows from an individual to a processor, Solove is more focused on the (negative) effect of information.

Perhaps we have even misunderstood the inherent limitations of property. That is what Berkeley Law professor Paul Schwartz has recently argued impressively. He maintains that the concept of property is sufficiently flexible and adjustable to work for information privacy. Key to his model of propertized information, which seeks also to fully safeguard information privacy, is an understanding of information property as a bundle of interests that can be shaped through the legal system. This permits law to limit certain kinds of trades, most notably any further use or transfer of information unless an individual has given her consent.[20]

These and many other reform proposals for information privacy have yet to be tried. But they already have fulfilled at least part of their purpose. They detail the shortcomings of some current information privacy rights setups, and prove that alternative rights frameworks not saddled with some of the drawbacks are possible—at least in theory. It is quite likely that over the next several years we will see even more innovative and refined alternatives proposed, and perhaps enacted. This is a space to watch—since individuals may have much to gain from improved information privacy rights.

However, the effectiveness of these proposals (as well as more traditional information privacy rights) depends not only on the capacity of the legal system to enforce them, but also on the willingness of individuals to bring action against perpetrators. To be sure, laws compare favorably with individual self-control because of their capacity to proscribe human behavior, particularly of information processors. By the same token, protecting one's information privacy rights may continue to be cumbersome and costly. Therefore, perhaps the idea of individuals controlling (and protecting) their information *would* work, if enforcement can be simplified. This is the promise of technical alternatives to the conventional legal mechanism of regulating behavior.

Digital Privacy Rights Infrastructure

Individuals are not the only group sensing an acute loss of control over their information. Intellectual property (IP) rights holders have been similarly battered over the last few years due to an onslaught of technical developments, outdated business models, and changed user behavior. Practically all of their content comes in digital format. Cheap storage, global broadband networks, and flat monthly connection fees paired with easy-to-use file sharing software have created what IP rights holders consider to be a nearly perfect storm: a majority of young people sharing content freely with each other and in defiance of existing copyright laws. The rights holders' response has long been multi-pronged. Tens of thousands of law suits against individual file sharers (and, at times, innocent bystanders) made headlines, but initiatives to embed copyright enforcement into technology arguably are both more important and pervasive.

The principle of what is often called digital rights management (DRM) is simple: information—in the context of copyright, these are music, movies, games, digital books, but in the context of forgetting, this could be any personal information—is paired with meta-information about who can use it and how. Media players check this meta-information and refuse to play information content if usage is not appropriately authorized. To avoid this content being played or copied using unauthorized equipment, often content and meta-information is encrypted requiring a special key that only authorized hardware devices "know." Unlike information privacy laws, therefore, DRM enforcement is based almost entirely on technology.

Rudimentary DRM systems have been with us for many years. Many commercial DVDs are encrypted as well as linked to a specific geographic region; one cannot play them without the encryption key or on a player from a different region. Similar systems have been devised for video games and video game consoles, like Sony's PlayStations or Microsoft's Xbox, as well as digital audio recording systems, from DAT to MiniDisc. For years, all music bought through Apple's iTunes Music Store had DRM meta-information embedded, limiting to which iPod one could download that song (it had to be "registered" with one's computer), or how often one could "burn" it onto a CD (seven times before one has to change the "playlist" of songs). Playing media on personal computers can be restricted through Microsoft's Media Player (in combination with the protected WMA format) and through RealNetwork's RealPlayer (together with RealPlayer's Helix format).

Unsurprisingly, therefore some have suggested utilizing the concept of DRM to ensure and enforce individuals' control over other types of information. NYU information systems professor Kenneth Laudon proposed creating a technical and organizational infrastructure through which individuals could "sell" the use of their personal information to vendors, and which would ensure enforcement of these contractual arrangements.[21] Cyberlaw visionary Lawrence Lessig echoed Laudon's ideas in his book *Code*, but suggested more specifically to use a DRM infrastructure developed for intellectual property rights to manage and enforce information privacy claims.[22] As such approaches tackle the challenge of an individual's control over her information, they may offer a suitable response to digital remembering as well. With such a system, individuals would add meta-data to their personal information detailing who can use it, for what purpose and price. Rules embedded in our computer's operating system would check this meta-data and ensure that a specific usage is permissible before processing an individual's information. As long as all or most technical equipment vendors embed the technical components of such a system into their devices, enforcement is ensured—even in jurisdictions that do not legally recognize information privacy.

Often opponents of DRM systems paint them as infrastructures of denial, focused on prohibition and control. That is—at least regarding Laudon's and Lessig's proposals—an unfair characterization. Technically restricting unauthorized usage of information is only one element of the systems they suggest. At least of equal importance is a technical and organizational infrastructure that enables those that want to use information to transact easily and efficiently with those that control access to information. The idea is to create markets of information in which usage transactions can take place at vastly lower cost than in existing markets, thereby not only enabling many more transactions but also offering a stronger incentive for rights holders to experiment with pricing structures. This could lead to more efficient markets for information, and thus be beneficial to society at large.

Such an approach has one important caveat, however, which proponents readily concede. While relying largely on technical mechanisms to ensure efficient transactions and effective enforcement, any such DRM infrastructure requires at least some support of the legal system, in particular in restricting attempts to circumvent the technical control mechanisms. In the realm of intellectual property laws, prohibitions on reverse engineering—included, for example, in the Digital Millennium Copyright Act—play that role.[23] For digital rights management to handle other information rights, reverse engineering restrictions would have to be extended accordingly.

And yet the DRM approach to protect and enforce an individual's control over her personal privacy has met with fervent and broad criticism, not all of it justified. Among the many and sometimes ideological arguments brought forward against DRM are three types that point towards severe practical and theoretical problems of digital rights management to handle such control.

The first problem focuses on how comprehensive a DRM system can be. For example, in the context of intellectual property, the information content can be encrypted and technically protected from its origin all the way to the end user. At that point, however, content must be made visible and audible for humans to enjoy, and thus leave the protected confines of the DRM system. At this "unencrypted moment," it can be recorded, creating an unauthorized and unprotected version that bootleggers can mass-distribute without technical restrictions. Of course, equipment manufacturers are trying relentlessly to minimize the unencrypted moment as much as possible. Thus, high-definition television signals travel encrypted even from the digital receiver box in one's home to high-definition TV sets. But all this technology cannot (yet) stop users from recording with a video camera a movie they watch, or taping a CD's tracks on an audio recorder. Of course, this reduces content quality (although excellent recording equipment produces copies of surprisingly high quality, which keeps content providers worrying). In the context of personal information, however, this problem may be much less severe. In contrast to copyrighted content that people want to watch or listen to—leading to an "unencrypted moment"—personal information is often used as input for information processing, and thus largely confined to perhaps a more protectable realm of a technical information processing infrastructure.

Opponents of DRM also argue that such systems will never be tamper-proof. Somebody somewhere will always break the technical lock used to protect information, even if laws prohibit such behavior. Once that lock is broken, information loses its protection. Past events seem to confirm this assessment. Over the years, methods have become easily available on the Internet to break all kinds of DRM systems, from those used on DVDs and PlayStation games, to those protecting Adobe's PDF files and Apple's iTunes songs. The situation resembles an arms race, in which ever-more complex DRM systems are eventually broken into by ever-more sophisticated opponents. The fundamental trouble with most DRM systems to date is that once they are deployed, they can no longer be altered in the face of a break in, leaving information content vulnerable. Worldwide device connectivity may alter this situation: once technical devices containing a certain DRM system are linked via the Internet, they can—at least in principle—be updated to iron out a weakness and block further break in. In the future, this may make DRM systems harder to circumvent.

There is another, perhaps more fundamental, concern to using DRM to control personal information. For a DRM system to work, it needs to follow what users are doing and stop them if they are trying to use information in an unauthorized way or for an unauthorized purpose. Leaving aside the question of whether and to what extent a technical system is able to grasp such an abstract notion as purpose, any system capable of making such judgment would have to watch how users handle protected information. In essence, it requires a technical system that continuously looks over the shoulders of users ready to stop an unauthorized activity. It would indeed be ironic if a DRM system protecting us from digital remembering would be implemented by creating a technical infrastructure of pervasive surveillance. A panopticon to protect us from a panoptic society? Perhaps technical innovation in the next couple of years can alleviate some of these concerns, but until then comprehensive and pervasive DRM systems continue to come with a frustrating birth defect.

There is a fourth challenge, centered on the need to specify possible usage, cost, and related conditions for each piece of information managed by a DRM system. Such meta-information is a prerequisite for the system to work. In the context of intellectual property rights, rights holders—often large commercial organizations—have strong incentives as well as trained staff to enter the meta-information and keep it up-to-date. In the context of personal information, the meta-data would have to be entered by individuals themselves. It is likely not an easy task to convince the average user to spend a few hours detailing usage policies, and to keep this meta-information up-to-date. And it is not just that entering usage polices is time-consuming for individuals. There is another difficulty. Describing how somebody else can use an image or a piece of music is relatively straightforward; describing under what conditions and for what purposes a piece of personal information may or may not be used is much harder, not the least because context and purpose matter so much. Current DRM systems use specific grammars and linguistic structures to describe how a particular piece of content can be used, and in return for what price. So far, these structures incorporate a relatively atomistic (not to say simplistic) view of what can be done with information, and disregard context and purpose; such structures would have to be quite radically improved to be adequate enough to help individuals capture the multitude of differing usages of personal information based on context and purpose efficiently and easily—a difficult task indeed. Imagine a simple example: if an individual were to specify the appropriate usage of her Social Security number, how exactly would she go about doing that, keeping in mind that sharing one's SSN is perfectly sensible for one purpose but terribly worrying in another, even if it is the same information processor requesting it?

There are two possible solutions to this important challenge. First, we could reconceptualize claims over personal information and model them similar to intellectual property claims. "Propertized" personal information has the distinct advantage of fitting much better into the grammar and structure used to describe permissible usage in current DRM systems. But as I mentioned earlier, quasi-property claims to personal information bestow on the "owner" near complete power to use the information as she pleases, eliminating any restrictions on information reuse. Individuals could decide whether they want to share personal information with others, but would have little control over context and purpose of future use. For copyrighted works, we have accepted such limitations. If I buy a book, I can read it at home or on the road, use it for my research, write notes in it, sell it to somebody else, or tear it apart. The copyright owner has little control over my using the book. Personal information we may want to treat quite differently: I may grant a particular processor of information the right to use my Social Security number only for a specific purpose and context. Standard property rights do not permit such fine-grained differentiation. They are blunt tools for what likely is too delicate a task. Moreover, as information privacy experts Paul Schwartz and Marc Rotenberg as well as intellectual property authority Pamela Samuelson and others have so eloquently pointed out, there are further reasons why standard property rights in personal information are not a good idea, although in our context perhaps the lack of fit is the most important.[24]

If making information privacy claims fit the technological infrastructure is not a good idea, the alternative solution would be to adapt technology to fit the concept of personal information control, and to create usage languages that more adequately describe an individual's choice of sharing her information for a specific purpose and under certain conditions. This is a tall order, and one not likely to be accomplished any time soon, but it may possibly be the only path forward in creating a technical solution—a DRM system—to manage and enforce individuals' control over their personal information.[25] Until then, such comprehensive DRM systems offer no help in finding a suitable response to digital remembering.

Perhaps though, we have simply envisioned DRM systems as too comprehensive and all-encompassing. Maybe a system offering a much less wide-ranging solution could be achieved using existing technology, while retaining efficiency. This is what Princeton information security expert Edward Felten and his colleagues have proposed: a "privacy management system" that facilitates negotiating usage and enforcement of control over personal information between two parties.[26] Unlike a pure property system, Felten's is based on direct and shared consent between the parties involved. Intriguingly, the system also allows the parties to keep their usage policies confidential, thereby insulating each other from outside pressure. It is an appealing and intriguing feature not found in conventional DRM systems that are based on transparency. The core beauty of the system, however, is that it does not require a central rights management infrastructure, and thus avoids building an infrastructure of surveillance. Such nifty ideas are useful antidotes to the danger of over-engineered solutions. Maybe limited "privacy management systems" in their ability to map existing information privacy behaviors and practices provide a more promising long-term path towards a workable technical solution that ensures personal information control.

In sum, whether comprehensive infrastructures or more limited systems, technical solutions offer some advantages over the previous two potential responses I discussed—digital abstinence and information privacy rights—but are also saddled with additional shortcomings. Where does this leave us? While each one of us may have a personal favorite, no clear winner emerged. Each approach has its strengths and weaknesses. Digital abstinence offers behavioral change without imposing external constraints—legal or technical—on individuals, but it is unclear whether it can tackle successfully the challenge of digital remembering. Information privacy rights represent a more structured and robust response, and one that has been successfully implemented in many jurisdictions around the world. But questions remain about its effectiveness. Technical systems to manage control over personal information pretend to solve the enforcement (and thus effectiveness) issue, but the rules required for technical systems to work, what behavior of information use is and is not permissible is surprisingly complex to formulate for experts, and likely intractable for the average individual, even if the other problems of such systems can be worked out. Each of these approaches represents a distinct mechanism of regulating behavior. Digital abstinence uses norms (and a bit of the market), information privacy rights rest on law, and rights management systems employ mainly technical architecture. In that sense, they seem to represent the paradigmatic approaches of behavioral modification that are available in our society.

Our interest in them, however, is narrow. Will they adequately and effectively address the challenge of digital remembering that we face?

Importantly, at their core they all are fundamentally relational. They all presuppose that the central challenge is information traveling from sender to recipient, from one human being to another, or from one organization to the next. They presume that the sender decides whether and under what conditions the recipient should use the information. Each of the responses aims at facilitating or shaping that relational condition of information sharing. This must not come as a surprise. All three approaches are rooted in the notion of information privacy, which at heart is a relational concept of constraining information sharing.

As I explained in the previous chapter, the challenge brought about by the demise of forgetting is twofold. The first is one of relative information power, of loss of control over information. The approaches I described, similarly relational, may be able to address this challenge. Whether they will also address the more societal danger of the spatial and temporal panopticon, I am less certain. Equally problematic is what I called the time challenge of digital remembering: that too much digital memory may overwhelm our human capacity to think, decide, and act in time, and to appreciate aptly our past—a threat that is decidedly not relational. The danger is less the information that others have about us, than our digital past impeding our abilities in the present. We are caught in it even without sharing information with anybody else, just like Jane was when reading her old e-mails. I am afraid relational approaches, represented by digital abstinence, information privacy rights, and privacy DRM, are not well suited to address this challenge. It is simply not what they have been designed for. Thus, as useful as these solutions may be to protect information privacy, they do not tackle directly the challenge of "time" that comprehensive digital memory poses.

Could there perhaps be a set of alternative responses that are less explicitly and exclusively founded on a relational concept, and thus better able to deal with digital remembering as an informational (rather than relational) issue? If we accept that digital memory—a set of information stored on digital media and thus frozen in time—is what our responses ought to address, a further, perhaps more fitting set of three possible approaches—based on norms, laws, and architecture—emerges.

This set of three responses is more speculative than the more familiar set of three I have just described. But as they focus less on the relational dimension of information, they may conceivably be better suited to address the "time" challenge of digital remembering.

Cognitive Adjustment

When my initial paper on the demise of forgetting in the digital age was discussed at Internet site Slashdot, Julian Togelius, an artificial intelligence researcher in Europe agreed with my diagnosis, but suggested a very different remedy. "Instead," he wrote, "we have to adapt our culture to the inevitable presence of modern technology. [...] We will simply have to assume that people can change and restrict ourselves to looking at their most recent behavior and opinions."[27] Togelius' sentiments were echoed by Harvard Berkman Center fellow danah boyd, who is convinced that "[p]eople, particularly younger people, are going to come up with coping mechanisms. That's going to be the shift, not any intervention by a governmental or technological body."[28] Togelius and boyd (and quite a number of others) do not deny that we are fast approaching a world that will not forget, but they believe humans will be able to adjust their cognitive processes to deal with digital remembering. It is a striking idea: permanent presence of all information would lose much of its sting if we could consciously disregard old facts and accept that humans are ever-changing beings, never locked into a particular state. Such cognitive adjustment would eliminate the potential danger of clouded decision-making or failing to act in time.

More precisely, cognitive adjustment is enticing for at least two reasons. First, it does not require changing society through the adoption of new laws, or the development and implementation of a novel technical architecture. Instead, the necessary changes take place in our minds. Second, by rewiring the way we think, evaluate, and decide, humans tackle digital remembering through adaptation, the very notion that is such a fundamental building block of life in general. This will resynchronize us with change—nature's most basic idea. We'll take care of the problem via the null hypothesis, by *not* trying to solve it through societal means. Eventually we'll adapt our cognitive mechanisms, enabling us to live in a world of digital remembering. Memory will be with us, but our adapted minds, much like a Teflon-coated pan, will disregard it before memory can confuse us.

Togelius and boyd are too smart to assume that such adjustment will come easily. I am sure they expect we'll go through a bumpy transition before things settle down, and we'll have acquired the cognitive upgrade we need. I agree. The real question is how long it will take. Unlike advocates of a rapid cognitive adjustment, I am skeptical such change is attainable within a couple of human generations. The views of leading psychologists bolster my skepticism. For example, David Schacter thinks that how humans manage memory and forgetting is not something that can be changed easily and at will, but rather is deeply rooted in the inner workings of our brain.[29] In addition, J. R. Anderson argues that how humans deal with time (especially through forgetting) is the result of a remarkably effective and useful adaptation over a long period of time to the contexts and environments they live in.[30] If humans could simply will to put memory into a temporal perspective, those who suffer from persistent memory (and cannot but recall trauma, for example) could be cured easily. Alas, so far the key to such an easy solution has eluded us. We cannot exclude that this will change, but from what we know today, it seems unlikely that in the shadow of digital remembering we can fast-track evolutionary adaptation and bring about a relatively sudden cognitive revolution.[31]

Suppose, however, we could in fact rewire our brains to the demands of digital remembering. Such cognitive adaptation would fail to address another fundamental downside of digital memory: that of incompleteness. Even in the digital age, not everything we communicate is captured in digital format—and certainly not what thoughts we ponder, and how we assess and weigh the pros and cons before making a specific decision. This incompleteness poses a problem when we revisit a decision much later in time. Going through digital memory will not provide us with the comprehensive context and complete set of information we need to reconstruct and thus understand what we decided in the past. Without such understanding, however, the past will continue to puzzle us, except if we cognitively adapt to this challenge as well, or of course if we disregard our past altogether. However, the moment we begin to weigh and evaluate which historic information to use and which to discount, we'll have to contend with (and be influenced by) the bias implicit in digital memory—of the preservation of information that can be digitized and the disregard of everything analog that cannot. It's unlikely that we will master this task by sheer cognitive discipline alone.

Proponents may argue that just like how enlightenment and modernity taught us to think critically, a few centuries from now humans will laugh at the difficulties of digital remembering that we face today because they will have learned successfully how to deal with it. That may be true, but I am not that interested in what will exist a few hundred years from now. I remain worried about how humans will cope with the decades of painful (and perhaps violent) adaptation in between. To be sure, my skepticism is conjecture, and the alternative—that humans adapt their cognitive abilities swiftly—while clearly improbable is not impossible. But unless we uncover additional reasons why cognitive adaptation—solving the informational problem of digital remembering at the level of self-controlling and self-correcting individuals—could work, searching for an alternative response to digital remembering may be a more fruitful strategy.

At its core, cognitive adaptation acknowledges comprehensive digital memory, then aims at limiting the influence digital memory has on our decision-making. If that is too ambitious a goal, because humans cannot help but take into account the information at their easy disposal, perhaps societal rules in the form of laws can limit what is committed to digital memory, and thus reduce the size of the information oceans that surround us. This leads us to the idea of information ecology.

Information Ecology

Information ecology is a deliberate regulatory constraint of what information can be collected, stored, and thus remembered, by whom and for how long. Recall the tragic case of the Dutch citizen registry. As the horrible outcome highlights, limiting what government can do with information in the registry does not protect against an uncertain future; however, *not* collecting and storing information in the first place does. Without information in the registry identifying religion and ethnic origin, the Nazis would have been unable to abuse the registry so repulsively. Restricting digital remembering not only ensures against actions of future external invaders, it also protects us from a future in which our own society may be tempted to utilize the information vaults of digital remembering to unduly profile, discriminate, and intimidate those who do not agree with the value preferences of the majority. We have all witnessed how in the wake of September 11, 2001, even very robust and strong democracies are tempted to accumulate and mine digital memory in the (often false) hope of better security.[32] As the Dutch case highlighted, collections of personal information are inherently risky, because we do not know how they will be utilized in the future. Rules of information ecology are antidotes to such perverse (re)use of information.

Information ecology rules, explicitly regulating how long information can be retained in digital memory, are nothing novel.[33] One encounters them as information deletion mandates in many different sectors and contexts. For example, when certain conditions are met (including lawful behavior and the passage of time) criminal records may be expunged—sealed or destroyed (although lately many jurisdictions opt for sealing rather than actual deletion of the information).[34] Similarly, after a period of time DNA information taken from witnesses or suspects that is no longer necessary in identifying and prosecuting the perpetrator of a particular crime is deleted from DNA databases at least in some states in the U.S.[35] Along the same lines, recently, in a rare unanimous decision, the European Court of Human Rights ruled that DNA information of innocent people cannot be retained forever, obliging the United Kingdom to change its laws and mandate information ecology.[36]

In addition to these sector- and context-specific rules mandating deletion and expungement of information, the general principle of information ecology has been included in many information privacy statutes. For example, Article 6 of the European Union Privacy Directive states that national laws must ensure personal information is "kept in a form which permits identification of data subjects for no longer than is necessary for the purposes for which the data were collected or for which they are further processed."[37] Such information ecology rules are not only found in formal laws, but also in privacy guidelines of companies developing information processing technology. The largest, Microsoft, has included information ecology prominently in its "Privacy Guidelines for Developing Products and Services." Under the telling heading "Reducing Duration of Data Retention," they state: "User Data should be retained for the minimum amount of time necessary to support the business purpose or meet legal requirements."[38]

The consequence of such rules is clear: personal information must be deleted once it has fulfilled its purpose. For example, credit card companies and telecom providers must scrub individual credit card transactions or records of individual phone calls from their digital memories once the respective bills have been settled (or at least erase the personal identifiers, like the name or account number of such records). To an extent, such mandated information ecology is a corollary of the purpose limitation principle: if personal information has been entrusted to somebody for a particular purpose, once the purpose has been fulfilled there is no further permissible way to use that information, and thus it must be deleted.

In the academic literature, suggestions for more stringent and comprehensive information ecology mandates have been advanced. Yale law professor Jack Balkin called for institutionalizing what he terms *government amnesia* "by requiring that some kinds of data be regularly destroyed after a certain amount of time unless there were good reasons for retaining the data."[39] And a few years earlier, my colleague David Lazer and I argued for a comprehensive set of information ecology laws, which we suggested would act as "information speed bumps," forcing information processors to slow down the tempo of information collection and storage.[40]

Whether sector specific or part of general information privacy statutes, such rules effectively enforce forgetting. Because they are legislative mandates directed at those storing information rather than requiring individuals to sue for enforcement, information ecology rules offer a more direct and effective response to the challenges posed by digital memory. Unfortunately, they come with two shortcomings. One is conceptual, the other political.

The conceptual weakness is that mandated information ecology is a comparatively blunt and binary tool. The issue of what information must be deleted and when is enshrined in laws and regulations, rather than—as with information privacy rights— the outcome of an individual's decision. This requires the setting of a general rule, rather than a flexible and adaptable one, since legal rules need to be precise with little room for interpretation. After all, people must be able to understand rules to follow them. Consequently, most existing information ecology rules constrain specific troubling cases—like DNA information— leaving unrestricted most other instances of digital memory that may similarly cloud our human capacity for rational decision-making; or they are linked to a relational concept of rights (such as Article 6 of the European Union Directive). The former limits the potential scope of information ecology norms, while the latter, as I have explained, fails to adequately address the "time" challenge posed by digital remembering.

The political weakness is that information ecology norms have had a very difficult time of getting enacted recently, despite the dramatic rise of digital memory. On the contrary, after 9/11 and during the ensuing "war on terror" rules prescribing the exact opposite—information retention rather than deletion—mushroomed. Banks have to collect and store information about individuals making international money transfers, ostensibly to help government interdict operations financing international terrorism.[41] All airlines flying passengers to the United States must provide dozens of U.S. law enforcement agencies with detailed personal information about each passenger, including address and credit card information in electronic format *before* the aircraft reaches U.S. airspace, so U.S. agencies can cross-check passenger data with (notoriously unreliable) databases of potential suspects (once even Senator Ted Kennedy ended up being included in such a governmental "no-fly" database).[42] Similarly, telecommunication providers in the United States as well as in Europe are now forced to retain transaction data of their customers' telecommunication connections for many months—even years—just in case law enforcement agencies decide they want to look at them.[43] Recently, I had to supply detailed personal information to enter a commercial flight simulator in Europe. Government now requires such records, too, to be collected and stored.

The rise of retention laws is caused by a confluence of different factors. First, the ostensible source of post-9/11 security concerns—worldwide terrorism—is hard to target directly. Terrorists are widely dispersed, have limited knowledge of the rest of their organization, and often act relatively independently. Despite some violent precursors in past decades, law enforcement agencies perceive global terrorism as a new threat, which they believe cannot be fought with the existing set of measures and tools at their disposal. This results in a shift in emphasis by law enforcement from solving crimes to preventing them. By the same token, law enforcement agencies have realized both how much information is flowing through the global information and communication networks, and how potentially valuable that information can be. There is a sense that if information is only correctly interpreted and correlated, terrorist activities could be detected successfully before the next attack takes place. Since agencies do not collect much of the relevant information, and often lack the storage capacities to keep such information, new information retention laws are seen as remedying this situation by forcing private sector companies to keep stored customer information in case law enforcement agencies want to access it in the future.

Whether this argument is valid or not, the recent renaissance of information retention laws not only reverses the progress towards forgetting that information ecology rules have achieved in earlier decades, but fosters a political environment that opposes information ecology. If government believes in broad and long-term retention of personal information for public security purposes (as it did during the tenure of President George W. Bush), it is unlikely government will aggressively enforce existing information ecology rules in the private sector.

There is another equally important reason why information ecology norms have fallen on hard times. To the string of recent corruption cases in the private sector, Congress responded with (among other measures) transparency rules, employing the same mechanism it used after Watergate, the public sector's most damning corruption scandal in past decades. Whether the unwieldy Sarbanes-Oxley,[44] the venerable Freedom of Information Act,[45] or the requirements to print nutritional information on foodstuff,[46] it seems transparency has become our preferred means for ensuring good governance, both in the public and private sector. This trend is palpable not just in the United States, but in many other societies as well. For example, environmental laws in the European Union include important transparency and self-reporting components,[47] and so do workplace safety regulations.[48] Even in nations with a limited tradition of transparency legislation, like Germany, policymakers have warmed recently to transparency rules, suggesting them for anything from manager salaries to politicians' board memberships.[49]

Although some academics have begun to caution against an overuse of transparency legislation, transparency continues to be seen by policymakers and public opinion alike as the mechanism of choice to reduce corruption and enhance oversight.[50]

Taken together, the renaissance of information retention laws and the surge in transparency rules reflect and facilitate a political climate opposed to information ecology regulation. That does not mean that individual lawmakers do not propose information ecology measures. For example, in 2008, Massachusetts State Rep. Bill Straus introduced a bill (H 4822) that would have mandated companies to delete behavioral marketing information (based on consumer preferences—what consumers shopped for when) after twenty-four months.[51] But the prevailing political climate has not allowed such information ecology rules to get enacted.

So far, we have looked at two distinct response strategies. One that constrains the amount of information in digital memory (information ecology), and a second that leaves digital memory unchanged, but advocates cognitively disregarding much of it. Each strategy is valuable, but neither offers a breakthrough. Cognitive adaptation seems too difficult to achieve for human beings, at least in the short term; and information ecology rules face both a hostile political climate and a lack of built-in flexibility. What underlies both approaches is that humans ought to limit the information they base their decisions on. Perhaps that assumption is flawed. A third alternative response, perfect contextualization, offers a drastically different perspective.

Perfect Contextualization

What if digital memory does not comprise too much information, but too little? So far I have suggested that as more and more information is added to digital memory, digital remembering confuses human decision-making by overloading us with information that we are better off to have forgotten. Consequently, we looked at possible responses to the threat of digital memory that are focused either on decreasing the flow of information from one person to another—the relational dimension underlying the first three approaches—or reducing the amount of information in digital memory—the information dimension at the heart of the last two strategies.

But as those for cognitive adjustment argue, aren't humans perfectly capable of evaluating conflicting information across time? Isn't that what we are constantly doing? Wouldn't cognitive adjustment work if we could only avoid the collection biases inherent in most digital memories? If all relevant information, including the context surrounding a past event is preserved in digital memory, and not (as is today) a relatively small subset of it, wouldn't we be able to adjust? Isn't digital memory only problematic if it selectively remembers information from the past, and thus provides its users with an incomplete picture?

This argument of perfect contextualization is not only a variation of the cognitive adjustment approach, it is also an extension of Brin's reasoning for a transparent society, in which comprehensive information about everything is (at least in principle) available to everyone, and individual information control has been replaced by general transparency.[52] To achieve such perfect contextualization we would need a technological infrastructure that collects, stores, and retrieves information about our lives much more comprehensively than exists today. We would need to abandon analog storage as well as unrecorded conversations, and we would have to become lifeloggers, just like Gordon Bell, retaining all the information we encounter and that we eventually use to make decisions. But we also have to go beyond Gordon Bell, and use the tools to share our information with others to achieve true and equal transparency. In short, we need the technical means for true digital remembering.

Information privacy experts may argue that perfect contextualization is creating a devilish infrastructure of surveillance. But as Oscar Gandy has reminded us, surveillance is about the asymmetric power to watch, a power that necessarily benefits the surveyor over the surveilled.[53] In a world where all information is transparent, Brin suggests, surveillance loses that power. And if the infrastructure of digital remembering could be organized in a decentralized fashion, much like the instruments Gordon Bell uses, perhaps no single entity, no matter how powerful, could ever hope to control all of it. Only somewhat tongue-in-cheek, lifeloggers have correctly pointed out that what they advocate is not surveillance (one watching another), but sousveillance (we watching us).

The argument, however, as I explained in chapter 4, has severe flaws. Total transparency is not necessarily benign. Brin suggests that such total transparency will take away our anonymity and make us all feel like we are living again in a small village, in which we'll behave because we are watched: "In the village, it wasn't fear of retribution, per se, that kept you from behaving callously toward your neighbors; it was the sure knowledge that someone would *tell your mother*, and bring shame to your family. Tomorrow, when any citizen has access to the universal database to come, our 'village' will include millions, and nobody's mom will be more than an e-mail away" (emphasis in the original).[54] Brin's reference to one's parent as a person of (relative) power brings his benign sounding metaphor right back to the kind of social control mechanism that is at the heart of Bentham's panopticon, of an oppressive architecture of surveillance. This is exactly why many are very reluctant to share their information with others. Even lifelogger

Gordon Bell is adamant about keeping his information treasures to himself.[55] If all have access to all information, it is likely some will have the technical, organizational, and economic means to combine and correlate the information better and further than others, resulting in a new landscape of the empowered and powerless, and not Brin's idealistic vision.

There are also theoretical limits to how much information even the best technical system can remember. If we trust in the completeness of information in such a system, we'll fool ourselves. For once, we are far from being able to digitally record the information that surrounds us. We'd have to make a quantum leap in technology diffusion and acceptance to reach a reasonably high level of comprehensiveness of digital remembering. And even if all communication and external information is recorded, digital memory will still miss an important source of information that (at least so far) cannot be digitized: our thinking. If only external information, but not our internal thoughts are remembered, digital memory will remain fundamentally incomplete (not to mention the limits the law of entropy places on how much we can store). As long as digital memory is significantly incomplete, it is not only not better than what we have today—human forgetting—but likely worse, in that the filtering process of what information gets stored and what gets discarded is not based on our mind's inner workings, or pure randomness, but rather biased by what our technological tools are able to remember.

Even if technically feasible, perfect contextualization requires sustained attention. To fully grasp a past decision, we would have to delve into a sea of digitally remembered information about it, including its context. Perfect contextualization may thus simply fail to offer us a comprehensive understanding of our past, because of the limitations of the human attention span.

Finally, perfect contextualization fails to address the second dimension—that of deciding and acting in time. As humans, we are captives of the linearity of time. It is impossible for us to jump back into our past, even if only as an accurate thought experiment, because we cannot undo the fact that we as human beings constantly learn, evolve, and change. Even if we are confronted with an exact record of a past event we were involved in, it would be impossible for us to block out the changes in our minds that have happened since: the knowledge gained (or lost), the values changed, preferences adjusted, emotions felt. We experience it when we read the same book a few years apart: we'll discover novel aspects, and interpret elements differently. Similarly, revisiting a previous decision even with perfect contextualization and infinite time will not enable us to retrace and thus understand the how and why of our original choice. Instead, we might be at odds with our original decision, wondering how we could have erred so starkly and acted so wrongly. Put simply, even if perfect contextualization may re-create the information context, it cannot take us back in time.

These weaknesses, when taken together, drastically reduce the value that perfect contextualization seems to offer, and make it a much less attractive response to the challenge of digital remembering.

I have now offered six responses to digital remembering. The first set of three was focused on the ability of individuals to control the sharing of information with others, reflecting the "power" dimension of digital remembering. The second set had at its heart the human process of using information for decision-making, echoing the "time" dimension. The responses in each set used a distinct mechanism to regulate human behavior: social norms and individual self-control, formal laws, and (technical) architecture. See Table 5.1.

TABLE 5.1. Potential Responses to the Demise of Forgetting

	Information Power (incl. information privacy)	Cognition, Decision-Making, and Time
Individuals	Digital abstinence	Cognitive adjustment
Laws	Privacy rights	Information ecology
Technology	Privacy DRM	Full contextualization

None of the six responses offered a silver bullet to counter the potential dangers of digital remembering, perhaps an indication of how intricate the challenge is we face, although each seemed to address a particular aspect of it. That the solutions proposed in the left-hand column of the table (addressing primarily the "power" dimension of digital remembering) seem a bit more developed and robust is not surprising. It is the result of decades of study, activism, debate, and enactment of measures to combat the perceived loss of information privacy. Nor is the relative weakness of solutions in the right column (addressing the "time" dimension) very startling. Only the recent rise of digital memory and the related demise of forgetting have brought this challenge to the fore.

Taken together, perhaps two conclusions are in order. The first is that to combat the dangers posed by digital remembering, it may require us to give up on finding a perfect answer, and instead pragmatically aim for a solution mix to ensure that all the necessary aspects of the challenge are addressed. The second conclusion is that coming up with additional creative approaches may be most valuable for the right column of our matrix, thus addressing the "time" dimension of remembering. One such approach is the focus of the following chapter.

CHAPTER VI

Reintroducing Forgetting

If we want to address the challenges of digital remembering, we may have to tackle the very shift that led to the demise of forgetting: where we used to forget over time, we now have the capacity to remember perfectly. Retaining information in our digital memories has become the default of how we operate, how we interact with our technical tools, and with each other. Today, remembering is so widespread I have argued, because it no longer requires a conscientious act, a tiny bit of time, energy, or money that we need to expend to commit information to digital memory. Digital forgetting, on the other hand, necessitates that extra quantum of human effort.

I suggest we reset this balance, and make forgetting just a tiny bit easier again than remembering—just enough to flip the default back to where it has been for millennia, from remembering forever to forgetting over time. We can aim to achieve this in many different ways. Let me sketch out one possible route—a combination of raised human and societal awareness, technical tools, and supporting legislation. To see how it differs from existing approaches related to information power and control, consider "cookies," the little information packets that web sites send us when we browse web pages to keep track of what we are doing.

A decade ago, I wrote an article on cookies.[1] In the piece, I explained that web browsers, like Firefox and Internet Explorer, can be configured to ask us to accept or decline an incoming cookie. But, I lamented, browsers won't tell us when they send a cookie with our information out to a web site, which, I criticized, happens clandestinely, and in clear violation of accepted principles of transparency and consent that are hallmarks of information privacy rights. Caught up in the conceptual world of such rights, I was alarmed that my web browser would not ask me before sharing my personal information with web sites (and thus remote information processors).

In light of digital remembering, however, I now realize that my reasoning then was incomplete. Just like the left column in Table 5.1 of the previous chapter, representing the first three responses I detailed, my argument was focused on the link between the user (or more precisely their web browser) and the information processor requesting information. It was rooted in the relational concept of information sharing, in a world of permission and consent. What it lacked was an appreciation of cookie warnings, the pop-up windows that let users decline an incoming cookie (rather than let them decide whether to share cookies with others). In essence, such cookie warnings help us limit comprehensive remembering by ensuring that some information does not even enter our digital memories. Moreover, these warnings of incoming cookies may annoy some users, but also raise awareness: the positive effect of continuously confronting users with the reality of an insatiable digital memory. Unlike a technical architecture of regulation like DRM, cookie warnings do not solve the problem *for* users, but rather confront users *with* the issue. Thus, cookie warnings bank on reminding users of the implications of cookies through frequent nagging.

As it turns out, cookie warnings are useful to limit digital memory. Their weakness is that they are extremely binary. User choice is "frontloaded"—when receiving a cookie, a user can decide whether it is sufficiently valuable to add to digital memory. But what if a user wanted to retain the cookie only for a limited period of time? It is more realistic to perceive of information not in binary terms (valuable or useless), but as being of value for a period of time, albeit not forever. Such a mechanism of deleting information at some future date (which cookie warnings fail to offer) could be more valuable, because it would create a less binary world of remembering and forgetting, enable more useful user choice, and follow more closely our human capacity to forget.

An Expiration Date for Information

One possible way we can mimic human forgetting in the digital realm is by associating information we store in digital memory with expiration dates that users set. Our digital storage devices would be made to automatically delete information that has reached or exceeded its expiry date.[2] In its most barebones form, this I believe may be sufficient to reintroduce the contours of forgetting, although numerous more sophisticated variations are conceivable to fit a society's specific needs and preferences. These variations, however, all share one core element. They are designed to confront us with (and thus remind us of) the "finiteness of information"—in other words, that information is inexorably linked to a point (or period) in time, and that over time most information loses its informational value, much like yesterday's newspaper, or an old joke we have heard too many times.

Users, when saving a document they have created, would have to select an expiration date in addition to the document's name and location on their hard disk. Users wouldn't be able to save the file without specifying an expiration date, much like how they can't save a file without selecting a name for it. Based on these preferences, the users' computers would do the rest: managing expiration dates and clearing out expired files, perhaps once a day. Of course, users would have a little software utility to change the expiration dates in case they discover information has lost its value earlier than expected, or remains important and useful beyond its originally envisioned lifespan. The paranoid may even have a tool that warns them when information is close to reaching its expiry date, so they can decide to adjust the date if they so desire. But by having our computers delete files that have reached the expiration dates we set (much like how we clean out foodstuff that has expired), we reintroduce forgetting into our daily routines, and shift the default back from pervasive remembering to human-controlled forgetting.

Much of the success (or failure) of expiration dates will hinge on user experience—on how easy it is for users to specify a suitable expiration date. The need to enter an expiration date should prompt users to reflect, at least for a moment, about the lifespan of the information they intend to store, but it should not annoy users with a cumbersome and complex user interface. Entering a date could be made easier by permitting users to choose a relative date (say, a month from today, or a year), as well as a carefully thought through selection of presets and defaults, perhaps based on the file type, the selected file location (some folders might hold files with a shorter lifespan than others), or even some (limited) semantic analysis of the file's content.

Expiration dates are not about imposed forgetting. They are about awareness and human action, and about asking humans to reflect—if only for a few moments—how long the information they want to store may remain valuable and useful. Perhaps in contrast to other responses (like digital abstinence or information privacy rights), expiration dates do not depend on overly idealistic visions of educated users abstaining from the Internet or suing for their information privacy rights. Nor are they based on an equally idealistic vision of a purely technical solution. Rather, powerful technical tools we have at our disposal are only utilized to remind us that the value of information is not timeless. Moreover, what is important is not that we are forced to choose, but that in doing so we have to reflect on the lifespan of information. As it will become part of our daily routines, we may realize what humans have at least implicitly grasped for millennia: that good information is preferable to copious information.

Technical Considerations

Technically (design challenges for the most appropriate user interface aside), expiration dates would be relatively easy to implement. They are just another type of meta-information associated with a piece of information (a document file in the earlier example). Our digital devices already manage and store an ever-increasing amount of such meta-information. File names and creation and modification dates are just three examples. Digital cameras, too, store meta-information with each picture taken, from shutter time and aperture to film speed. Most cameras add the date and time when an image was taken, too. Soon we'll see geographical meta-information (longitude and latitude) added to our media by our GPS-enabled cameras (and phones). Our music library software manages meta-information for our music tracks, from name and band and genre to links to lyrics and album art and playlists, to our own keywords ("tags") and preferences. And yes, the DRM systems built into most of our media players similarly provide (and enforce) meta-information of usage rights for copyrighted digital works.

Meta-information is not confined to our computers and gadgets. An abundance of it drives much of what we call Web 2.0: on the Internet we tag stories and rate blog posts; we recommend sellers and comment on Wikipedia entries. These all are types of meta-information linked to and associated with some piece of information on the Web. Expiration dates would simply add another type of meta-information to digital memory: "information about information's life expectancy" if you wish. Much like other meta-information (think of digital images), the expiration date would be made to "stick" to the information it refers to, ensuring that if one copies a file, the expiration information is copied along with it. And in the background, a small software application would regularly clean out expired information. On many of our digital devices, the framework of such functionality is already present. For instance, our personal computers automatically clean our hard disks of information and auxiliary files no longer needed on a daily or weekly basis. Discarding expired files could be just one additional housekeeping task that is performed.

To ensure the presence of the technical architecture (and thus the necessity for humans to set expiration dates) requires the help of the law, mandating that the devices we use to store digital information include code to support information expiration dates, require users to enter such an expiry date when saving digital information, and discard automatically information that has expired. It would not be the first law to prescribe the functioning of software. Existing statutes already constrain software by requiring mechanisms or processes for the protection of information privacy or intellectual property, by compelling software manufacturers to conform to certain principles of security and reliability (from digital signatures to voting machines to flight control systems), or even mandating that software conforms to certain ergonomic principles.[3] This would just add one more requirement, and would be a relatively simple one to implement.

The Role of Information Processors

Expiration dates limit the amount of information companies, and even the government, may have available on consumers and citizens. This they may find troubling. However, they may still come to embrace expiration dates. Today, commercial and governmental information processors maintain huge information repositories, but have little clue which pieces of information in these repositories are still valid and valuable, and which ones have long become outdated. Left without a clear signal of information validity, processors like Google or Amazon resort to complex algorithms to approximate what information to use when providing services from web searches to book recommendations. The inherent imprecision of such guesswork leads to erroneous results (book recommendations or web search results far off a user's current preferences) and lost sales, or in the case of government law enforcement, it may cause false arrests. With an expiration date in place, information that has shed its value could be weeded out of digital memory, leaving processors with a significantly improved information base to use. And because primarily users, not processors, set expiration dates, such a potential increase in information quality may cost processors little if any money.[4]

Individuals also trust online service providers to not abuse the personal information they have stored. If online service providers violate that trust, individuals may switch to alternative providers. That applies even to Internet heavyweights.

Columbia law professor Tim Wu puts it quite bluntly when he comments, "as soon as you lose trust in Google, it's over for them."[5] Competitors, too, may use a trust violation incidence to communicate their comparative advantage. Of course, switching providers entails cost. Such costs vary depending on the context. Switching to a new e-mail account can be quite difficult—one has to inform friends and colleagues, perhaps reprint business cards, or even learn new e-mail software. Switching search engines, on the other hand, is likely less painful.[6]

Online service providers like Google, Microsoft, or Yahoo! are acutely aware of that. In 2007, Google announced that it would begin to anonymize (and thus delete personal information from) search queries.[7] It did so at least in part to preserve its customers' trust. Just a few months earlier, Google had come close to violating that trust. In 2005, the U.S. Department of Justice had requested hundreds of thousands of search queries from leading web search companies.[8] While most other web search companies complied without much fuss, Google fought the request in federal court. It eventually won, but feared it might not be able to fend off subsequent requests.[9] That put the search giant in a quandary. It had built its fortune around the concept of digital memory, and had stored almost every bit of information it ever obtained. This made it a prime target for any governmental agency in need of massive user information. Already, users around the world began to feel uneasy about Google's power. Any massive sharing of user information with the U.S. government would endanger its customers' trust in Google, which the company had spent so long and hard to build. To keep that trust (and thus its position as the Internet's leading information intermediary), Google's management saw little choice but to side with its users and fight the government's request. But that was winning a battle, not the war. To position itself to maintain user trust long-term even if government agencies would succeed in obtaining search query data, in the spring of 2007 Google decided to implement a general expiration date on search queries: personal identifiers in them would now automatically be deleted after a maximum of twenty-four months.[10]

Google's announcement, however, gave its competitors an opening to challenge the Internet search giant by offering even shorter expiration dates. In the summer of 2007, Microsoft and search web site Ask.com jointly announced they would discard search queries after eighteen months, undercutting Google by 25 percent.[11] Around the same time, Yahoo! announced it would discard personal identifiers from search queries after thirteen months, almost twice as fast as Google.[12] Later that year, Ask.com even implemented a version of the expiration date mechanism on its web search page. With one simple mouse click, users could delete their search history whenever they wished. And in July 2008, new search engine Cuil declared it would not store personalized search queries at all.[13] By September 2008, Google countered, announcing it would forget personal identifiers in search queries after nine months.[14] This competitive dynamic offers an encouraging lesson for an expiration date for information: as concerns over information retention among users rise, information processors dependent on user trust might have to adjust their offerings.

For some companies, like Google, the changes that expiration dates mandate may require some technical work, perhaps even modification of business practices. For others, it may do no more than reflect their existing privacy commitments. Take Microsoft, for example. Its exemplary "Privacy Guidelines for Developing Software Products and Services" state that "[u]ser Data should be retained for the minimum amount of time necessary" and "[a]ny User Data stored by a company should have a retention policy that states how long the data should be kept and the manner in which it should be removed from all data stores."[15]

Expiring Information Bits

So far, I have described how an expiration date could work for information files. There are circumstances, however, where a more fine-grained approach is preferable. Cookies offer a case in point. All cookies that are sent to web browsers are stored in a dedicated cookie file on user computers. But each cookie's useful lifespan is different from that of others. It thus makes sense to choose an expiration date separately for each cookie rather than for the entire cookie file. Intriguingly, the standard describing cookie meta-information already foresees expiration dates for each cookie. All that is needed is a simple way for users to set that date when a cookie is received (and perhaps a chance to update the date later).

Amazon.com offers another illustrative example. Its book recommendations are based on one's previous book purchases and book browsing. Amazon already offers its customers a way to exclude specific earlier book purchases from the information base used for recommendations. But users have to locate and navigate to a specific web page to do so. It would be much easier if at the time of purchase customers are given a chance to enter an expiration date for such transaction information. For example, if they were ordering birthday presents for somebody else, they might opt for a short expiration date, so future recommendations for them wouldn't be "tainted" by their purchases for somebody else. And if one was ordering books for an upcoming trip or a specific exam, one might select the day of departure or exam as a useful expiry date, resulting, again, in reduced digital memory as well as improved future recommendations. Asking customers to specify an expiration date at the time of purchase (when the information is added to the customer file) offers two advantages to the current system. First, one-off purchases for others could be quickly filtered out of the recommendation base. Second, in the context of a purchase, customers likely have a better sense of how long they envision they will be interested in a particular topic or author than having to remember to revisit this question many months later.

Web search sites, like Google Search, Microsoft Search, Yahoo! or Ask.com, could similarly implement an expiration date both for web page links and web search queries. Let's discuss web page links first. Currently, web search engines "crawl" through the Internet. They do this mostly by following links from one web page to another. Any new page discovered that way will be added to the search engines' index, and a copy will be stored in case it isn't reachable (what Google calls "caching"). This way, with huge computing power and enormous storage facilities, web search engines build a gigantic catalogue of what is available online. As the content of the web constantly changes, search engines must continuously crawl the web to keep its information up-to-date. In very simple terms, web pages contain content to be shown in a web browser, and instructions on how to visually render and present this information. Because of the importance of search engines in locating content, web pages also often contain meta-information for search engines, suggesting keywords for indexing its content. One such meta-information tag can be used to ask search engines to *not* index and cache a particular page, thereby excluding it from digital memory. This is already enabling forgetting, albeit in a very binary form.

Instead of such a stark either-or, one could envision a new meta-information tag with which web page authors define how long search engines keep the link to a particular web page in their index and/or its content cached. Because the technical infrastructure to interpret such meta-information for search engines is already in place, adding another meta-information tag would be relatively easy and straightforward to implement. As a consequence, web page authors could select how long their information remained relevant. In addition, web search engines could even display the expiration dates next to the search results as a crude but useful indication to users of a search result's relative value.

Expiration dates also could be used for search queries. Upon entering a search query, users could be prompted to input an expiration date, or could select one from suitable presets. Users searching at somebody else's computer, or performing a one-off search for a colleague or friend, for example, would select a short period, while those researching for their long-term interests would choose the opposite. Users would have to pay a tiny cost—the time to reflect, decide, and click—but in return they would get vastly more control over their search history (and more relevant results in future searches) as well as reduce digital memory.

Web search sites would store the expiration date with the search query and handle the information accordingly, including automatically deleting the record of that specific search request when its expiration date has been reached. Quantitatively, search sites would lose some of the search query information they use to fine-tune the ranking of search results, but the quality would likely improve as less relevant past queries are omitted.

Potential application for expiration dates may even go beyond the confines of personal computers or online services, and include emergent technologies. For example, recently the European Union discussed the implications of RFID (radio-frequency identification) chips and similar networked sensing devices that add information to our digital memories. The Council of the European Union concluded to promote "the possibility of deactivating RFID chips or any other way which provides empowerment and user control."[16] Instead of the relatively stark "silencing of the chips" that the Council suggests, perhaps mandated expiration dates might offer a somewhat finer-grained approach.

As these cases highlight, introducing an expiration date for information does not require individual users to learn complex new user interfaces. But designing such easy-to-use interfaces is both a challenge and a necessity. If expiration dates are to catch on, users must be able to set them easily—a quick thought and an extra mouse click or two should be all that's necessary. And the level (files or smaller pieces of information like individual cookies) at which expiration dates are employed could depend on the type of information and the usage context.

Reviving Forgetting, Not Solving Information Privacy

In chapter 4, I laid out the potential dangers of digital remembering, using the terms "power" and "time." A number of suggested responses to digital remembering that I detailed in chapter 5 are based on mechanisms developed to ensure information privacy. I have made clear that the challenges posed by the demise of forgetting are not congruent with those being addressed by information privacy. My suggestion for a revival of forgetting, perhaps through expiration dates, aims at tackling the "time" challenge of digital remembering. The goal of expiration dates for information is to reduce the amount of information that is digitally remembered. Insofar as this limits the amount of information that can be shared with others, expiration dates may have a net positive effect on information privacy. But I must emphasize that expiration dates do *not* solve more general concerns about control over information that arise in relational contexts, when information is shared between two or more parties, and which we most commonly call information privacy, confidentiality, or intellectual property issues. The demise of forgetting and the threats to information privacy are two *complementary challenges* that require complementary responses. As much as I think expiration dates can help ease the challenge of digital remembering, they can never supplant mechanisms guaranteeing information privacy.

A Spectrum of Options

The examples I have outlined represent implementations of an expiration date for information in different settings and contexts. What they have in common is that they raise awareness of the temporal dimension of information, set an expiration date before committing information to digital memory, and have discarded automatically information that has thus expired. But beyond this skeletal structure, vastly different versions of expiration dates for information are conceivable, depending on the type and context of the information in question. Equally important, concrete implementations of an expiration date for information also must reflect differing societal preferences. These preferences find their expression in legal structures and rules, as well as the technical architecture we choose. Different societies will differ in these preferences, much like how they differ in what information privacy and intellectual property laws they enact and enforce—and the law facilitating expiration dates are the mechanism through which these differences are played out.

I envision at least two fundamental dimensions through which these societal preferences will be expressed. Based on these two dimensions, different implementations of expiration dates can be constructed, depending on how information with expiration dates is shared in a society. The first such dimension signals a society's inclination for how permanent and "sticky" an expiration date is, while the second reflects who a society believes should set an expiration date.

Persistence of Expiration Dates

As I have explained, an expiration date is meta-information that is linked to the piece of information to which it refers. Societies only wanting a minimum of protection against digital remembering may simply mandate that expiration dates must remain connected to that information. In such a system, the recipients of information would be free to alter the expiration date if not limited by contracts or other rules. Technically, such an implementation constrains information processing only minimally. In terms of awareness, social norms and market pressure—alternative mechanisms of influencing human behavior—may have an impact on behavior through preference signaling, even in this weak system. Suppose users select expiration dates, and then share that information with other parties. If these information recipients openly disregard their customers' preferences, including the longevity of a piece of information expressed through expiration dates, customers may take their business elsewhere. Of course, this depends on how costly it is for consumers to switch to alternative providers, and whether such providers exist.

If a society wants to go beyond that minimum, lawmakers may mandate that expiration dates generally persist—that is, they can only be changed by the originator or with her explicit consent. Such a rule may sound familiar. It's a sibling of the purpose limitation principle of information privacy statutes. In essence, an expiration date is an instance of purpose limitation, a restriction of information to a particular use, one that takes place before information expires. Even under such a relatively strict system, credit bureaus and direct marketing database vendors will continue to operate, but it may force them to think a bit harder about their information collection and retention policies. Similarly, it may push operators of computerized reservation systems in the travel industry to delete records after a reservation was cancelled, and not retain them for much longer, as is currently their practice. Plus, government agencies may have to consider whether and when to delete citizen data, rather than keeping everything stored.

There may be some situations in which individuals are not best suited to choose expiration dates themselves—for example, when individuals are unaware of the potentially harmful consequences of setting too long or too short an expiration date. In such situations, lawmakers may set upper ceilings for expiration dates, or mandate fixed expiration dates for certain types of information and/or certain kinds of transactions.

Discussing such legislative options of persistent expiration dates with engineers, especially outside the United States, I have often heard them voicing concerns over the effectiveness of a legal mandate. They are concerned that the law is an inadequate mechanism to enforce "stickiness," and point to what they see as similarly ineffective information privacy laws. Wouldn't it be better, some of them argue, to use technology to ensure persistent expiration dates? Instead of prohibiting information processors from changing expiration dates without an individual's consent, legislation could mandate the use of DRM to ensure persistence of expiration dates. Information containing expiration dates could be digitally signed, rendering unauthorized change in the expiry data—for example, by a third party—significantly more difficult. Of course, to avoid circumvention of DRM, such a legislative mandate would also have to prohibit the unauthorized alteration or tampering of expiration date information, similar to the much-criticized Digital Millennium Copyright Act.[17] Perhaps technically securing the persistence of expiration dates makes sense for particularly sensitive types (or contexts) of information. But largely for reasons that I have detailed when analyzing DRM architectures in the previous chapter, I remain skeptical of approaches that aim at eliminating the human factor and promise perfection. After all, the core goal of expiration dates for information is precisely not to push the problem of digital memory off our consciousness by delegating it to technology, but rather the opposite: to make humans aware of the value and importance of forgetting.

Negotiating Expiration Dates

So far, I have explained how expiration dates for information would work when an individual is committing a piece of information to digital memory. In many instances, though, information refers to more than one person. Take an ecommerce transaction, for example: the information generated is linked to both buyer and seller. Who of the two sets the expiration date? In essence, this reprises the information control debate, but shifts it from who has control over the information, to who controls the expiration date of it. The question of how to decide for jointly generated information may seem similar to the issue of persistence I just detailed. In both cases, the question is one of control. But there is a fundamental difference. Persistence is about the preservation of an expiration date once it has been set. When information is jointly generated, however, no expiration date has yet been set, and both parties may have similarly valid claims to partake in deciding it.

So which party is to decide? Both. In principle, each transactional partner could determine independently the expiry date for information before committing it to digital memory; one would not need to be bound by the expiration date choice of the other partner(s). Superficially, this would achieve little. If a buyer can disregard the expiration date for the transactional information set by the seller and vice versa, neither Google nor Amazon nor any other such information processor would have to change operations, and forgetting would continue to be the exception, not the rule. Yet, even such a weak implementation of expiration dates could possibly yield an (albeit small) net positive effect, similar to what I outlined for stickiness. By confronting users with the need to specify an expiration date for the information they save, awareness could be raised. Perhaps individuals would come to expect that expiration dates will be accepted and valued by their transactional partners. To the extent individual customers are willing and able to translate these expectations into market preferences—choosing transactional partners based on whether they honor one's expiration dates—information processors desiring to retain customers would have to adjust their policies.

For a more stringent approach, a formal legal rule could mandate that expiration dates are to be set jointly, so that all parties involved have to use the same expiration date for the same piece of information. Thereby, individuals would know the expiration date of information they jointly generated, like book purchase records or web search queries. Such transparency paired with awareness of the dangers of digital remembering could assist individuals in negotiating expiration dates jointly with transactional partners. In the context of Amazon's book purchase records, for example, Amazon could offer customers a date range from which they would pick a suitable date. Of course, negotiations about expiration dates are part of general transactional negotiations, and if transactional partners can't agree on a joint expiration date, there won't be a transaction. That may hurt vendors, too, not just consumers, especially in difficult economic times.

But mounting market pressure may be too idealistic a vision. Jointly set expiration dates presuppose that transactional parties have roughly equal negotiation power—an unlikely situation, as I explained in chapter 4. Individuals may often be in an inferior bargaining position when they negotiate expiration dates, and they may also face limited choices in expressing their dissatisfaction. It is a common phenomenon in information markets: while there are dozens, even hundreds of vendors, less than a handful capture most of the market. More so than elsewhere, in sectors built on networks, success begets more success (due to network effects), thus creating a strong pull towards a dominating vendor. On the other hand, switching costs for consumers tend to be lower than in some traditional settings, perhaps offsetting some of the unequal negotiation power and capture effect of large information processors. The remaining power imbalance may make lawmakers want to offer a more gradated solution to jointly generated expiration dates. Especially contexts with gross imbalances of negotiation power may warrant attention. A number of options are available. For example, depending on the context, laws could set ranges or an upper limit of permissible expiration dates, or mandate that in certain contexts or for certain transactions, processors must accept expiration dates set by their customers (an option that may appeal to European nations and their consumer protection legislation).

Negotiations over joint expiration dates could possibly be facilitated by technical architecture—for example, by utilizing mechanisms similar to the intriguingly simple yet powerful system Ed Felten and his colleagues suggested (and which I described in chapter 5).[18] For users, such negotiations would not necessarily have to involve a complex give and take. Consider the following scenario regarding taking photos and videos. Suppose somebody takes a digital picture of you. If seen as an information transaction, the expiration date for such a picture ought to be set jointly between the picture taker and yourself. Rather than haggling over it in person, the negotiations over expiration dates could be done electronically. Each digital camera could have a built-in process to select expiration dates (perhaps through an easy preset). Before taking a picture, the camera sends out a "picture request." Imagine further that we carry with us small "permission devices" (the size of key rings) that when receiving such a "picture request" respond with the owner's preferred expiration date. The device could even have a little selector to quickly change preset expiration dates, perhaps from "zero" (if one does not want the picture added to digital memory at all) to "three years from now" (a medium term duration) to "100 years from now" (for memorable events). When the picture is taken, it's stored with the shortest of all expiration dates received (including that of the picture taker himself). The camera could even provide a visual cue as to whether somebody's device said "zero" or similar extreme compared to others in the picture. Such a solution could be easy enough to utilize for most users, and yet make it possible that pictures we do not want stored long term would become forgotten over time.

As is obvious, expiration dates are not a one-size-fits-all solution. A whole range of options are conceivable, from a barebones implementation of the core idea to more complex and far-reaching versions. Different implementations may vary widely, and no version is inherently better than the others. Which version a society selects depends not just on the type and context of information, but also on society's preferences and values, as well as the institutions at its disposal to enforce it.

Expiration Dates Compared

Compared with alternatives, expiration dates for information may offer some advantages. Unlike digital abstinence, they embrace participation in digital culture and global networks. In contrast to information privacy rights, expiration dates do not depend solely on individuals fighting costly and time-consuming battles in court. Neither do expiration dates require a comprehensive technical infrastructure of control, like DRM systems, as well as functioning markets in personal privacy to emerge. Compared with digital abstinence, information privacy rights, and DRM systems, expiration dates have the advantage that they are not a means conceived to solve a different problem—information privacy—repurposed to combat digital remembering. Expiration dates are designed primarily to address the "time" dimension of digital memories, and to limit the amount of irrelevant information stored. Expiration dates do require widespread awareness, but not a cognitive revolution. They are broader than information ecology mandates, and much more limited than an architecture of full contextualization.

Expiration dates are a modest response to the demise of forgetting, in at least four ways. First, technically, they utilize many of the ideas, infrastructures, and mechanisms that already exist, and in many instances would require limited technical modifications. Second, legally, they introduce to the digital realm the default of forgetting that is so familiar to us in our analog world, without relying on new rights or new institutions. Third, expiration dates are also modest in their combination of mechanisms regulating human behavior, including law and software. And fourth, politically they may be more palatable than a comprehensive regulatory approach and certainly less controversial than intrusive DRM systems.

In one important aspect, though, expiration dates may be seen as radical: they aim at changing the default of remembering in the digital age. Since forgetting is central to human decision-making, such an adjustment has significant consequences on how our digital lives are shaped.

Reintroducing forgetting through expiration dates is also saddled with a number of perceived, as well as actual, shortcomings. For example, some may dislike expiration dates because they do not solve all challenges of information privacy. This is true. But as I have mentioned they are not intended to.

Second, expiration dates may be accused of impeding the work, and even calling into question the very existence, of archives and libraries. This belief is unfounded. Expiration dates let individuals decide how long they want information to be remembered. But societies have the power to override such individual decisions if necessary—for example, by mandating information retention, and by maintaining libraries, archives, and others special institutions to preserve the information about a particularly important event of the past. Nothing of this proposal would alter or change that—except perhaps the need to make such information retention exceptions explicit and transparent.

Third, and more generally, tensions will remain between an individual's desire to forget and a society's desire to remember (and vice versa). In societies that cherish the individual over the collective, as a concededly crude rule of thumb, individuals should be the ones to set expiration dates. However, in certain cases societal concerns may outweigh individual preferences. For example, recently courts in Europe had to decide whether the names of past Communist informants could be published, or whether two decades after the end of the Cold War they should be afforded the benefit of oblivion.[19] This is a decision that expiration dates do not and cannot preempt; it is one societies must make. If, for instance, a society desires to inhibit forgetting about a defining event of its past, it can mandate (long-term) expiration dates, or exempt certain information archives from honoring expiration dates altogether. As long as such mandates are the exception, rather than the rule, they are entirely consistent with the vision of expiration dates, and with the more general idea of forgetting by default.

Fourth, expiration dates for information do not guarantee perfection. In the absence of a technical lock-down that makes impossible the circumvention of the expiration dates mechanism, leakages—information disconnected from expiration dates to circumvent deletion—will persist, albeit of varying degree. But as legal theorists have long maintained, perfect enforcement is not necessary to achieve widespread compliance. It is sufficient to have some enforcement, especially if a rule is widely accepted in society. If circumvention of expiration dates is frowned upon in society, enforced by law, and made harder through limited technical measures, resulting compliance may be sufficient.

Fifth, as I explained earlier, expiration dates are not immune to differences in information power. For example, when expiration dates are being jointly set by two or more parties, the more powerful may push the less powerful to agree to an expiration date. Lawmakers may need to carefully craft a supporting legal framework that counters (or at least reduces the frequency and severity of) such outcomes. I previously suggested some possible elements of such a legal framework. But even with a supportive legal framework, some unequal outcomes may persist. Without question, this is a weakness of expiration dates.

However, it may not be a crippling one. The primary aim of expiration dates is to address the "time" challenge of digital remembering, not the "power" challenge. Other measures aimed at addressing the "power" challenge of information in general may aid in creating more equal negotiation positions over expiration dates. Expiration dates may be combined with some of the other responses I detailed in chapter 5, especially those that address the "power" challenge of digital remembering. Equally important, expiration dates (as I have mentioned) reduce the overall amount of information others store about us, thus constraining the information power others may have over us. This in turn may make negotiating expiration dates more equitable.

Sixth, much of the success of expiration dates will depend on how easy and intuitive it is for users to set them. Expiration dates will only become accepted if they are not seen as an annoyance but as a valuable reminder that most information is not timeless.

Seventh, in its most simple form, expiration dates suffer from a structural weakness. They are binary in nature: information remains accessible before the expiration date, and completely inaccessible thereafter. There is no gradual decay, no process of losing details about a past event before forgetting the core of it. In that sense, expiration dates work differently than the mechanisms of forgetting in our human brain.

To an extent that is inevitable. We do not know well enough yet how human forgetting and recall work to replicate them with sufficient precision in digital code. But that should not keep us from trying. Perhaps it is possible to craft an expiration date mechanism that is a bit closer to how human memory and forgetting work, in return for only a modicum of added complexity.[20] For example, we could make our digital storage devices aware of how often an individual recalls a particular piece of information over time, and have our devices adjust the digital lifespan for items that are often recalled. That way they would mimic human memory, in which often recalled information is remembered much easier (and longer) than information rarely queried. Similarly, information processors could provide users with visual cues that indicate how close a piece of information is to its expiration date, and thus make it easier for users to devalue information that is close to the end of its lifespan, and to focus instead on more relevant information (as signaled through its expiration date). Introducing such temporal cues is, I believe, one of the next big steps in improving web search and online services, and introducing expiration dates furnishes information processors with the necessary technical infrastructure to do so.

Even more promising in the long term may be digital versions of a "rusting" memory that mimics partial as well as gradual forgetting. We could envision, for example, that older information would take longer to be retrieved from digital memory, much like how our brain sometimes requires extra time to retrieve events from the distant past. Or digital memory might require more query information to retrieve older information, mimicking how our brain sometimes needs additional stimuli for us to remember. A piece of digital information—say a document—could also become partly obfuscated and erased over time, and not in one fell swoop, thus resembling more closely human forgetting and partial recall.

It is important that we continue to theorize and experiment with these more elaborate and complex systems of digital forgetting. Compared with these sophisticated means of forgetting, expiration dates are crude. But in the absence of more sophisticated means today, expiration dates may offer a valuable first step towards a more forgetting world.

This chapter focused on reintroducing forgetting in the digital age, an additional possible response to the potential threats posed by digital memory, addressing in particular what in chapter 4 I termed the "time" challenge. Many possible approaches exist to put digital forgetting in place. One such way to reintroduce forgetting is to implement expiration dates to revive the default of forgetting. Expiration dates work well for many types of information and in different contexts, and offer a number of advantages over other approaches. They aim at raising human awareness and empowering individuals, require relatively little technical change, and by weeding out the outdated and irrelevant they perhaps increase the overall quality of digitally stored information. Expiration dates offer the implementation flexibility that societies with their different preference and value sets require. In the long run, expiration dates may even have a net positive effect in reducing information power differentials, and facilitating information privacy. Most importantly, though, expiration dates gradually lift the burden of comprehensive digital memory from our shoulders, and ensure that humans and society retain their ability to "act in time."

Expiration dates do come with weaknesses, however. They do not guarantee perfection, and cannot ease the tension between individuals wanting to forget and a society desiring to remember (or vice versa). Insofar as they rely on joint decisions, differences in information power are not overcome, and likely require additional measures (including legislation) to address. Their long-term success critically depends on easy-to-use yet efficient user interfaces. Finally, expiration dates are relatively binary in nature (when a date is reached, information is deleted). In the future, we may want to replace it with a (yet to be conceived) more sophisticated and gradated mechanism of forgetting, permitting the "rusting" or "decaying" of information over time. More generally, it is important to understand that expiration dates are no panacea. I am suggesting them not to replace all other responses to digital remembering, but to complement them, adding their specific set of strengths and weaknesses to create a potent combination.

Whether or not expiration dates in particular, and forgetting in the digital age in general, will become implemented depends largely on us. Are we individually as well as a society willing to take the necessary steps? This will require sustained debate to define the exact mechanisms and to build public support. It may even require a movement of sorts, much like the one to reform copyright laws. Perhaps first steps for such a movement are already under way. For example, in Argentina, writer Alejandro Tortolini and his colleague Enrique Quagliano have initiated a campaign to "reinvent forgetting on the Internet."[21] They have appeared on television, radio, and in print media, and continue to advance their ideas helped by surprisingly robust public support.

While this is heartening, much much more remains to be done in many societies the world over to increase public support and to establish expiration dates as a viable potential complement to other responses in our quest to revive forgetting, and thus help humanize our digital age.

CHAPTER VII

Conclusions

As humans we do not travel ignorantly through time. With our capacity to remember, we are able to compare, to learn, and to experience time as change. Equally important is our ability to forget, to unburden ourselves from the shackles of our past, and to live in the present. For millennia, the relationship between remembering and forgetting remained clear. Remembering was hard and costly, and humans had to choose deliberately what to remember. The default was to forget. In the digital age, in what is perhaps the most fundamental change for humans since our humble beginnings, that balance of remembering and forgetting has become inverted. Committing information to digital memory has become the default, and forgetting the exception.

Digitization has made possible plummeting storage costs, easy information retrieval, as well as global access to digital memory. For the first time in human history, this has enabled us to make remembering cheaper and easier than forgetting, to reverse the age-old default. It is easy to see why. In the face of our own often failing human memory, wouldn't we all opt for total recall? Wouldn't we all want to preserve our thoughts and impressions for posterity? And so we find ourselves in a "brave new world" of comprehensive digital memory, in which information processors like Google offer the world access to millions of billions of characters of information, from photos and blog posts to detailed marketing information and high-resolution satellite imagery of our (and our neighbor's) backyards. Soon, cases like Stacy Snyder's and Andrew Feldmar's will become common occurrences: lives shattered (or at least dented) by perfect recall of trivial past deeds, individuals exposed to a strangely unforgiving public, not just in North America but around the world. In fact, during the writing of this book, a minor conservative politician in Germany was fired from his job because his page on a Facebook-like system showed that in his past he had joined online groups with questionable names and content.[1]

In chapter 3, I explained why this trend should concern us for two important reasons. First, it transfers power from the surveilled to the surveyors, as information privacy experts have eloquently pointed out. But it does so across time. As digital memories make possible a comprehensive reconstruction of our words and deeds, even if they are long past, they create not just a spatial but a temporal version of Bentham's panopticon, constraining our willingness to say what we mean, and engage in our society. Do we really want to live in a society of servility and fearfulness? Second, forgetting performs an important function in human decision-making. It permits us to generalize and abstract from individual experiences. It enables us to accept that humans, like all life, change over time. It thus anchors us to the present, rather than keeping us tethered permanently to an ever more irrelevant past. Plus, forgetting empowers societies to be forgiving to its members, and to remain open to change. Digital remembering undermines the important role forgetting performs, and thus threatens us individually and as a society in our capacity to learn, to reason, and to act in time. It also exposes us to potentially devastating human over-reaction—a complete disregard of our past.

We must respond to the challenges posed by digital remembering—and I believe we can, by reviving our capacity to forget. I am not advocating an ignorant future, but one that acknowledges that with the passage of time humans change, our ideas evolve, and our views adjust. We can respond to the shadow of digital remembering employing a variety of different means. In chapter 5, I outlined six of them—two sets of three. In each set, one response fostered forgetting through social norms, laws, or a technical architecture. The first set of responses (derived from information privacy debates) addressed primarily what I termed the "power" challenge of digital remembering, while the second set targeted the "time" challenge, and thus arguably more directly the demise of forgetting. While all six strategies hold some promise and offer insights into the complexity of the problem we face, none of them provides us with a silver bullet. To effectively counter digital remembering, we may have to combine them, perhaps even add further responses.

In chapter 6, I suggested one such additional response: to reintroduce the concept of forgetting in the digital age through expiration dates for information. The aim is to shift the default back from retaining information forever to deleting it after a certain amount of time. I described the various structural, legal, and technical components of expiration dates and how they would work together. I offered a spectrum of possible implementations based on how thoroughly policymakers and the public desire to revive forgetting. Expiration dates are relatively modest on a number of implementation dimensions, making them comparatively easy to adopt. And yet they may be enough to stop and reverse the shift towards remembering and restore our capacity to forget, which is so central to what it means to be human. While I believe in the validity of enabling forgetting through expiration dates, I acknowledge that they too come with inherent weaknesses, and fail to address all problems of remembering. Pragmatically speaking, however, they may turn out to be what we need—the missing complement to our existing set of responses.

Most importantly, though, I want us to commence a wide-ranging, open, and intense discussion about forgetting, and how we can ensure that we'll remember its importance in our digital future.

Notes

Chapter 1. Failing to Forget the "Drunken Pirate"

1. *Snyder v. Millersville University et al.*, (mem.)(Dec. 3, 2008), http://voices .washingtonpost.com/securityfix/Decision%202008.12.03.pdf. Stacy Snyder sued her university in federal court. Once close to being settled, the case eventually progressed to the U.S. Federal District Court for Eastern Pennsylvania. In December 2008, Stacy Snyder lost her case when the court held that the photo and caption she posted on MySpace was not protected by the First Amendment.
2. Isaac Arnsdorf, "Seattle Attorney Finds that the Internet Won't Let Go of His Past"; Andrew Levy, "Teenage Office Worker Sacked for Moaning on Facebook about Her 'Totally Boring' Job"; Associated Press, "Naked Photos, E-mail Get Teens in Trouble," *Fox News.com*.
3. Steven Musil, "Facebook Hits 175 Million User Mark."
4. See Lenhart, and others, "Teen Content Creators," *Pew Internet & American Life Project*.
5. Howard, "Analyzing Online Social Networks," 14–16.
6. Palfrey and Gasser, *Born Digital*.
7. Liptak, "The Nation's Borders, Now Guarded by the Net," *The New York Times*.
8. For an intriguing fiction story along similar lines, see Cory Doctorow's *Scroogled*, September 17, 2007, http://blogoscoped.com/archive/207-09-17-72.html.
9. Associated Press, "Naked Photos, E-mail Get Teens in Trouble."
10. Null, "Drunken Pirate Says 'Be Careful What You Post Online'"; Liptak, "The Nation's Borders, Now Guarded by the Net."
11. The functioning of MAD was detailed in a half-hour Spiegel-TV television documentary on German television channel VOX; "Discofieber in der Provinz," Spiegel-TV, January 15, 2008, 10:15 pm, VOX, see http://www.spiegel.de/sptv/extra/0,1518,527060,00.html.

12. According to the FAQs on their web site, the management of MAD also uses the data they collect from their guests to throttle the number of non-Germans permitted in the disco; a shocking reminder that information is a power used to control others, which includes the power to discriminate.

13. Helft, "Google Adds a Safeguard on Privacy for Searchers," *The New York Times.*

14. In March 2007, Google had first shortened the retention period to eighteen to twenty-four months, and in September 2008 it more than halved the retention time to nine months; see Helft, "Google Tightens Data Retention Policy–Again," *The New York Times.*

15. ComScore Media Advisory, "Baidu Ranked Third Largest Worldwide Search Property by comScore in December 2007."

16. See Microsoft, "Privacy Principles for Live Search and Online Ad Targeting."

17. See Hasbrouck, "What's in a Passenger Name Record (PNR)?"

18. See Solove, *The Digital Person*, 20; for an earlier account, see Garfinkel, *Database Nation.*

19. Solove, *The Digital Person*, 21.

20. See Lazer and Mayer-Schönberger, "Statutory Frameworks for Regulating Information Flows," 368, 371.

21. Zick, "Clouds, Cameras, and Computers," 15.

22. *BBC News*, "CCTV Boom 'Failing to Cut Crime.'"

23. See Rosen, *The Naked Crowd*, 22; Heymann, *Terrorism, Freedom, and Security*, 104; Rule, *Privacy in Peril*; see also Kreimer, "Watching the Watchers: Surveillance, Transparency, and Political Freedom in the War on Terror," 133–82; Balkin, "The Constitution in the National Surveillance State," 3–12; Lee and Schwartz, "Heymann: Terrorism, Freedom and Security," 1463–68.

24. See, for example, the GPS Snitch, and Blip from BlackLine GPS Inc.

25. The first digital camera with a built-in GPS was the Ricoh Caplio G3, but Sony, Pentax and others have followed suit. Today, many smartphones, including notably the iPhone 3G, combine GPS and a digital camera.

26. *The Economist*, "The Hidden Revolution," 18.

27. See, for example, Griswold, *Forgiveness–A Philosophical Exploration.*

28. Miller, *The Assault on Privacy.*

29. Viktor Mayer-Schönberger, *Generational Development of Data Protection*, 219; see also Bennett, *Regulating Privacy*, 46–60; Flaherty, *Protecting Privacy in Surveillance Societies*, 21–30.

30. Bentham, Panopticon (Preface), 29–95.

31. Gandy, *The Panoptic Sort*. On the information panopticon, see Whitaker, *The End of Privacy*, 32–46; Rule, *Privacy in Peril*; Slobogin,

Privacy at Risk; see also Rosen, *The Naked Crowd*, and Rosen, *The Unwanted Gaze*.

32. Westin (*Privacy and Freedom*) and Miller (*The Assault on Privacy*) are often described as the fathers of the privacy debate in the U.S. The early theorists in Europe include Spiros Simitis, Wilhelm Steinmüller, and Adalbert Podlech. See Flaherty, *Protecting Privacy in Surveillance Societies*. The leading legal treatise in the U.S. is Solove, Rotenberg, and Schwartz, *Information Privacy Law*. For an excellent and comprehensive analysis of the politics of decades of privacy legislation, see Bennett, *Regulating Privacy*, and more recently Diffie and Landau's *Privacy on the Line*; see also Solove, *The Digital Person*; Cate, *Privacy in the Information Age*; Rosen, *The Unwanted Gaze*; Rule, *Privacy in Peril*. For a comprehensive anthology focused on recent privacy challenges, see Agre and Rotenberg, eds., *Technology and Privacy*.

33. See Borges, *Collected Fictions*.

34. See Foer, "Remember This,": 32–55; the article is based in part on Parker, Cahill, and McGaugh, "A Case of Unusual Autobiographical Remembering," 35–49.

35. Parker, Cahill, and McGaugh, 35.

36. Lasica, "The Net Never Forgets," *Salon*.

37. See, for example, Blanchette and Johnson, "Data Retention and the Panoptic Society: The Social Benefits of Forgetfulness," 33–45. See also Bannon, "Forgetting as a feature, not a bug: the duality of memory and implications for ubiquitous computing," 3–15; Bellia, "The Memory Gap in Surveillance Law," 137.

Chapter 2. The Role of Remembering and the Importance of Forgetting

1. On this and the following, see Baddeley, *Human Memory: Theory and Practice*.

2. For an instructive description, see Deering, *The Limits of Human Vision*.

3. The human ear has about 12,000 sensory cells. Nerve cells can fire up to 500 times a second. Thus, doing a simplistic calculation, the ear could produce as much as 6 million bits of information every second. See Smith, *The Scientist and Engineer's Guide*, 352.

4. Baddeley, *Human Memory: Theory and Practice*.

5. Bredenkamp, *Lernen, Erinnern, Vergessen*, 59–60. There is one small exception: Information that is acquired without explicit attention may be able to bypass short-term memory to reach long-term memory, but this is

not the intentional memorizing of sensory stimuli that we refer to when talking about remembering and forgetting.

6. It is likely that procedural memory is captured through different biological processes compared with declarative memory; see *The Economist*, "H.M.," Dec. 18, 2008, 146.

7. Wixted and Carpenter, "The Wickelgren Power Law and the Ebbinghaus Savings Function," 133–34.

8. Schacter, *How the Mind Forgets and Remembers*, 134.

9. See Berg, "Remembering Every Day of Your Life."

10. This is simply another way to state that, in regards to entropy and information, as randomness increases so does the information in the system, and vice versa. Since memory is information, no additional information can be gained in a system without an increase in energy.

11. McNeill and McNeill, *The Human Web*.

12. Ibid., 14.

13. Carruthers, *The Book of Memory: A Study of Memory in Medieval Culture*.

14. Plato, *Theaetetus*, and Plato, *Phaedrus*, Michael Rossington and Anne Whitehead, eds. (Baltimore, MD: The Johns Hopkins University Press, 2007), 25–27.

15. See, for example, Aristotle, *De Moria et Reminiscentia*, Michael Rossington and Anne Whitehead, eds. (Baltimore, MD: The Johns Hopkins University Press, 2007), 28–38.

16. The Grotte Chauvet is perhaps the most important, and the cave paintings of Altamira in Spain the most stunning.

17. Schmandt-Besserat, *How Writing Came About*.

18. See Kilgour, *The Evolution of the Book*.

19. Ibid., 18–19.

20. For the story of the library of Alexandria, see Kilgour, 20–21; Casson, *Libraries in the Ancient World*, 9–16.

21. For the debate, see as an example Fish, *Is There a Text in This Class?* and Eco, *Lector in Fabula*.

22. Casson, 126.

23. Casson, 88–92.

24. Drogin, *Anathema! Medieval Scribes*, 15.

25. See Dillenz, "Druckprivilegien und Drucker zwischen Kapitalismus und europäischem Religionsstreit," 46–49.

26. Schramm, "The Cost of Books in Chaucer's Time," 39–145. The calculation is actually a bit more complex, since Schramm reports costs in 1933 U.S. dollars. These can be adjusted to 2008 U.S. dollars using the CPI calculator of the Federal Reserve Bank of Minnesota, online at http://woodrow.mpls.frb.fed.us/Research/data/us/calc/index.cfm.

27. Drogin, 37; see also Yu, "Of Monks, Medieval Scribes, and Middlemen," 1–31.

28. Eisenstein, *The Printing Revolution in Early Modern Europe*, 14.

29. Febvre and Martin, *The Coming of the Book*, 186.

30. Eisenstein is cautious to add that such rough calculations are "inevitably open to dispute." They nevertheless provide us with a sense of the size of the revolution then under way. See Eisenstein, 13.

31. See Febvre and Martin, 143–59.

32. Anderson, *Imagined Communities*, 39. Anderson notes that, astonishingly, Luther's books account for a third of all German-language books sold between 1518 and 1525. See also Edwards, *Printing, Propaganda, and Martin Luther*, 21.

33. Schaff, *History of the Christian Church*, 5.

34. Febvre and Martin, 112–15 and accompanying notes; see also Martin, *Print, Power, and People in 17th-Century France*, 407–8.

35. Kilgour, 67.

36. On the production process, see Febvre and Martin, 71–75.

37. See Man, *The Gutenberg Revolution*, 113; in detail, see Lee, *The Social and Class Structure of Early Chosun*.

38. Kilgour, 111.

39. Ibid., 112.

40. Ibid., 99; see also Graff, *The Legacies of Literacy*, 303–14.

41. Eliot, "Never Mind the Value, What about the Price," 188.

42. Ibid., 165; Kilgour, 112.

43. The most famous description and analysis of these spaces of public discourse is found in Habermas, *The Structural Transformation of the Public Sphere*.

44. The situation was somewhat different in the United States, where owners of local printing presses often published local newspapers to provide them with a much-needed additional revenue stream. Far away from global news, those living in North America desired newspapers as a connection to the rest of the world. See Febvre and Martin, 211.

45. Starr, *The Creation of the Media*, 48.

46. Anderson, *Imagined Communities*.

47. See Loke, "Photography Review; In a John Brown Portrait." The current price was calculated using the unskilled wage data series, see Williamson, *Five Ways to Compute the Relative Value*.

48. Leggat, *A History of Photography*.

49. For example, in 1938, a movie camera might have sold for USD 29.50, the 2006 equivalent of USD 906. These and other historic prices I use are taken from two wonderful archives: the Newspaper Archives at http://www.newspaperarchives.com; and the Morris County historic prices archive, available online at http://www.gti.net/mocolib1/prices/.

CHAPTER 3. THE DEMISE OF FORGETTING—AND ITS DRIVERS

1. Wilkinson, "Remember This?–A Project to Record Everything We Do in Life"; see also Gaudin, "Total Recall: Storing Every Life Memory in a Surrogate Brain"; Thompson, "A Head for Detail," 94–114.
2. Gaudin, "Total Recall."
3. Cited in Zachary, *Endless Frontier*, 265.
4. Zachary, 261–62.
5. See Bush, "A Vision of Hypertext," 172.
6. Lyman and Varian, *How Much Information?*
7. Digital systems do not have to be based on the binary code. One of the first computers, the Mark I, designed by Harvard's Howard Aiken and IBM, did not utilize the binary code, using instead the decimal one. Neither did the ENIAC. (Aiken switched to the binary system in later machines.) See Cohen and Welch, eds., *Makin' Numbers–Howard Aiken and the Computer*; see also Jan Van der Spiegel et al., "The ENIAC," 130–32.
8. Analog NTSC television images have a resolution of about 440 by 486, compared with 1920 by 1090 for full high-definition digital television.
9. Brown and Duguid, *The Social Life of Information*.
10. Vaidhyanathan, *The Anarchist in the Library*.
11. A comprehensive comparison chart of hard disk costs can be found at http://www.littletechshoppe.com/ns1625/winchest.html.
12. This reduction in storage cost/increase in storage capacity has been termed Kryder's Law. See Walter, "Kryder's Law."
13. Gordon E. Moore, "Progress in Digital Integrated Electronics," 243.
14. Flash memory chips also use technology to ensure that all parts of the chip are used roughly equally, so no part wears out quicker. This spreading of the wear extends lifetime significantly.
15. This may be different for businesses running extremely popular interactive web sites if they want to preserve most or all of that sea of data produced.
16. Wilkinson, "Remember This?"
17. For some time, experts argued that either technology or market pull was driving innovation. Studies have shown that in many instances both factors were important. This is especially so for the semiconductor industry. See Mowery and Rosenberg, "The Influence of Market Demand," 193.
18. I am assuming an hourly cost of USD 16 (based on the current average annual personal income of USD 32,000 and 2000 working hours).
19. See, for example, Schulman, "What Was gwb@whitehouse.gov Really Up To?"
20. See, for example, Greewald, "What Does Sarah Palin Have to Hide in Her Yahoo E-mails?"

21. See Pear, "In Digital Age, Federal Files Blip Into Oblivion," *The New York Times*.
22. See, for example, Berman, "Got Data? A Guide to Data Preservation."
23. See http://www.gmail.com.
24. comScore Media Advisory, "Baidu Ranked Third Largest."
25. See Schroeder and Gibson, "Disk Failures in the Real World." For an analysis of Google's hard disks, see Pinheiro, Weber, and Barroso, "Failure Trends in a Large Disk Drive Population."
26. In fact, information on a hard disk drive even survived the catastrophic disintegration of Space Shuttle Columbia. See Minkel, "Hard Disk Recovered from Columbia Shuttle."
27. See, for example, Oakley, "E-Beam Hard Disk Drive Using Gated Carbon Nano Tube Source and Phase Change Media," 245–50.
28. John Markoff, "H. P. Reports Big Advance in Memory Chip Design," *The New York Times*, May 1, 2008.
29. Markoff, "Redefining the Architecture of Memory," *The New York Times*.
30. Eisenstein, *The Printing Revolution*, 64–73.
31. Kilgour, *The Evolution of the Book*, 76–77.
32. Ibid., 94–95.
33. Cole, *Suspect Identities*.
34. Michael R. Curry, "Location and Identity: A Brief History," 157; see also Michael R. Curry, "Toward a Geography of a World without Maps"; Rose-Redwood, "Indexing the Great Ledger."
35. See Telegeography, *Global Bandwidth Research Service*; see also OECD Directorate for Science, Technology, and Industry, *Broadband Statistics to June 2007*; see also Atkinson, Correa, and Hedlund, "Explaining International Broadband Leadership."
36. "Raw Data," *Wired*. See also Fay, "Worldwide Fiber and Cable: Demand, Production, and Price."
37. New Paradigm Resources Group, "Dark Fiber: Means to a Network," 6. In 2008, Telegeography estimated that about ten to twenty percent of long-distance fiber was lit; see Telegeography, *Global Bandwidth Research Service*.
38. Bakos and Brynjolfsson, "Bundling Information Goods"; see also Shapiro and Varian, *Information Rules*, 73–78.
39. It is important to note here that for a typical broadband connection, downloads to a user are faster than uploads from that user to the network. This is a result of the configuration of the network and is based on what broadband providers perceived to be an asymmetric usage pattern of users: they download more information than they upload. However, more recently these asymmetries have become much less pronounced, and broadband providers work at offering more symmetric transfer capabilities.

40. Gaudin, "Total Recall."
41. Lenhart et al., "Teen Content Creators."
42. See Krebs, "Teen Pleads Guilty to Hacking Paris Hilton's Phone," *The Washington Post*.
43. BBC News, "Identity 'at risk' on Facebook."
44. Watzlawick, Beaver, and Jackson et al., *Pragmatics of Human Communication*, 48–71.
45. Nozick, *Philosophical Explanations*, 584; although even Nozick suggests that such digital memory should not be kept forever, and that humans "want there to be some time after which you continue to leave a mark."

CHAPTER 4. OF POWER AND TIME—CONSEQUENCES OF THE DEMISE OF FORGETTING

1. This is the promise of what Manuel Castells has termed the "flexible production economy." See Castells, *The Rise of the Network Society*, 154; and HarrisInteractive, *The Harris Poll #4*. According to the Harris Poll, 59 percent of consumers are uncomfortable with web sites that tailor their content or ads based on a person's preferences.
2. This rests on the view that where information asymmetries persist, markets could become inefficient. Buyers could end up with low-quality goods they paid too high a price for—an inefficient allocation of resources. And if buying again, they may choose a good with the lowest price, knowing they do not know quality (see Akerlof, "The Market for 'Lemons': Quality Uncertainty and the Market Mechanism," 488–500). Or market participants could hide some of their qualities to obtain a good or service at a price they otherwise would not be able to. Third, market participants could hide their intention to change their behavior when it is the basis of the transaction (think of a person who begins to drive recklessly after having taken out comprehensive car insurance). These problems, it is argued, can be overcome by more and more symmetrical information, which is what online market makers have tried to achieve utilizing digital memory.
3. Michael Spence, who won the Nobel Prize with George Akerlof, is the author of a theory of signaling he originally developed for the job market, and which—in a much adapted form—eBay's reputation system is an example of. See Spence, "Signaling in Retrospect and the Informational Structure of Markets," 434–59.
4. See New York City Department of Health and Hygiene. *Restaurant Inspection Information*, http://www.nyc.gov/html/doh/html/rii/index.shtml. Also see *BBC News*, "Dishing the Dirt." For an excellent analysis, see Fung, Graham, and Weil, *Full Disclosure*, 50–93.

5. The U.S. Environmental Protection Agency, *Window to my Environment*, http://www.epa.gov/enviro/wme/; U.S. Environmental Protection Agency, *Toxic Release Inventory*, http://www.epa.gov/tri/. For general information on the toxic release inventory (but not its GIS version online), see Fung, Graham, and Weil, *Full Disclosure*, 50–93.

6. See Graham, *Democracy by Disclosure*, 21; see also, generally, Roberts, *Blacked Out*.

7. See Burkert, "Freedom of Information and Electronic Government," 125–41. Burkert pointed out that this may cause tension between people as consumers of government services and people as citizens of our society.

8. A plethora of web sites have cropped up in the United States and elsewhere providing voters easy access to information on political donations, board memberships, and lucrative consulting jobs. See, for example, *MAPlight.org Money and Politics: Illuminating the Connection* at http://www.maplight.org. Recently, cyberlaw pioneer Lawrence Lessig decided to join the fray by launching the Change Congress movement that makes transparent "pledges" that politicians take on campaign finance; see http://change-congress.org. Whether, and to what extent, such additional transparency fosters democratic engagement, as well as improved election outcomes, is a hotly debated subject. See Stiglitz and Florini, *The Right to Know*. For a somewhat critical view, see Fung, Graham, and Weil, *Full Disclosure*.

9. For an early analysis, see Resnick and Zeckhauser, "Trust Among Strangers in Internet Transactions," 127–57.

10. See, for example, Dellarocas, "Analyzing the Economic Efficiency of eBay-like Online Reputation Reporting Mechanisms"; Cabral and Hortacsu, "The Dynamics of Seller Reputation"; Gillette, "Reputation and Intermediaries in Electronic Commerce"; and Houser and Wooders, "Reputation in Auctions: Theory and Evidence from eBay," 353–69.

11. Hansell, "Sellers Give Negative Feedback on eBay Changes," *The New York Times.*

12. "As part of our continuing efforts to respond to Homeland Security issues . . . starting April 1, 2002, Direct Connect access will no longer be available to the general public. Direct Connect access to Envirofacts will only be available to U.S. EPA employees, U.S. EPA Contractors, the Military, Federal Government, and State Agency employees." OMB Watch, *EPA Email to Direct Connect Users*; see also U.S. Environmental Protection Agency. *Envirofacts Data Warehouse*, http://www.epa.gov/enviro/html/technical.html#Accessing.

13. There is a debate as to how effective the elimination of direct access to the EPA Envirofacts database was in preventing terrorists from obtaining information, especially since much of it can still be accessed, albeit with

greater effort. For a critical view of the clamp down, see Baker et al., *Mapping the Risks*.

14. This, of course, is posing the question of interpretative consistency. See Eco, *Lector in Fabula*.

15. Bacon, *Religious Meditations*, "Of Heresies."

16. See Rose, *Authors and Owners*.

17. Statute of Anne, 8 Ann., c.19 (1709) (Eng.).

18. See Keohane and Nye, Jr., "Power and Interdependence." For an extension of this view, see Mayer-Schönberger and Brodnig, "Information Power: International Affairs in the Cyber Age."

19. Miller, *Assault on Privacy*, 185.

20. See Lasica, "The Net Never Forgets," *Salon*.

21. For a modern version of this proposal, see Zittrain, *The Future of the Internet*, 228–29.

22. The question of the value of ties based on the topology of one's network is but one area in which network theory has recently rendered important insights. For a learned yet eminently readable introduction, see Burt, *Brokerage and Closure*.

23. Mayer-Schönberger and Lazer, "From Electronic Government to Information Government," 1–14.

24. Westin, *Privacy and Freedom*; Miller, *The Assault on Privacy*.

25. I have tried to provide a larger legal framework for capturing this human desire to control information; see Mayer-Schönberger, *Information und Recht*.

26. *U.S. Department of Justice v. Reporters Committee for Freedom of the Press*, 489 U.S. 749 (1989), at 762; see also Kreimer, "Watching the Watchers," 161.

27. For official details, see http://www.usps.com/ncsc/addressservices/move-update/changeaddress.htm.

28. An FTC investigation in 2007 concluded that such undisclosed access violated federal law, but no fines were imposed. see *BusinessWeek*, "They Know What's in Your Medicine Cabinet."

29. *BBC News*, "CCTV Boom 'Failing To Cut Crime.'"

30. See Kopelev, *To Be Preserved Forever*.

31. Bhatti and Singh, *Spock*.

32. See Gorman, "NSA's Domestic Spying Grows as Agency Sweeps up Data,"; Blanchette and Johnson, "Data Retention and the Panoptic Society, 39; Balkin, "The Constitution in the National Surveillance State," 13.

33. Brin, *The Transparent Society*.

34. Friedman, *Guarding Life's Dark Secrets*, 11.

35. Schacter, *How the Mind Forgets and Remembers*.

36. Ibid., 129.
37. See also *The Economist*, "Everybody Does It."
38. The talk was part of the Google sponsored *Personal Democracy Forum 2007*, New York, available online at http://www.youtube.com/watch?v= ut3yjR7HNLU.
39. And as the exact line between permissible and prohibited content continued to change, it further encouraged self-censorship. Few have resisted. For an example of a member of the elite who turned into a powerful and artful dissenter under difficult circumstances, see Maron, *Flugasche*.
40. For an illustrative enactment, see Mühe, Tukur, Koch, and Gedeck, *The Lives of Others*.
41. Foucault, *Discipline and Punish*.
42. Wagenaar, "My Memory: A Study of Autobiographical Memory over Six Years."
43. A recent study seems to suggest differently. Through computer simulations, the authors suggest that some brain cells do encode memories using relative time. See Aimone, Wiles, and Gage, "Computational Influence of Adult Neurogenesis on Memory Encoding."
44. Borges, "Funes, His Memory," 137.
45. Ibid.
46. Proust, *In Search of Lost Time*.
47. As quoted in Foer, "Remember This," 53.
48. Price, *The Woman Who Can't Forget*, 42.
49. Starbuck, "Unlearning Ineffective or Obsolete Technologies," 725–37.
50. For a wonderful exposition of how reading is forgetting, see Bayard, *How to Talk About Books You Haven't Read*, 55–57.
51. King, *The Commissar Vanishes*.
52. Orwell, *1984*, 171–72.
53. See *Wikipedia: Researching with Wikipedia*, http://en.wikipedia.org/wiki/Wikipedia:Researching_with_Wikipedia; see also Doctorow, *Scroogled*.
54. Priedhorsky et al., "Creating, Destroying, and Restoring Value in Wikipedia."
55. On the former, see Harris, *Selling Hitler*. A wonderful example of retouching photographs to alter the past can be found in King's *The Commissar Vanishes*.
56. Some may suggest that we use technology to ensure the authenticity of our digital memories. This may be valuable, but it is unclear how we would go about doing so—and how we would ensure that digital memories were unalterable even for those in charge of authentication.
57. Eliot, *Burnt Norton*, no. 1 four quartets.

CHAPTER 5. POTENTIAL RESPONSES

1. On the neo-Luddite movement, see Jones, *Against Technology: From Lud-dites to Neo-Luddism*; for a neo-Luddite view, see Glendinning, *My Name is Chellis*.

2. Palfrey and Gasser, *Born Digital*, 66–69.

3. Ibid., 53–59.

4. Benkler, *The Wealth of Networks*.

5. One more intriguing version of digital abstinence is for individuals to use multiple online identities that are neither linked to each other nor to the real-world identity of the person. This would enable individuals to com-partmentalize information streams by making it hard for information processors to combine bits of personal information into one comprehensive picture.

6. These two potential challenges for digital abstinence "light" also apply to the use of multiple online identities since information processors may require individuals to identify themselves not through one of their pseudo-anonymized online identities, but through one that links to a person's real-world identity. Moreover, once enough information bits point to the same online identity, the real-world identity of that person can be uncovered.

7. Warren and Brandeis, "The Right to Privacy." For a recent argument to revive the privacy tort, see Blackman, "Omniveillance, Google, Privacy in Public."

8. Solove, Rotenberg, and Schwartz, *Privacy, Information, and Technology*, 11.

9. Public Law No. 93–579, 88 Stat. 1897 (Dec. 31, 1974), in part codified as 5 U.S.C. § 552a.

10. Rubinstein, Lee, and Schwartz, "Data Mining and Internet Profiling," 273. Of course, there are (a) sector-specific information privacy rights that cover many more recipients of information (see, for example, the Health Insurance Portability and Accountability Act–HIPPA, Pub. L. 104–191, 110 Stat. 1936), (b) state laws guaranteeing information privacy rights in certain circumstances, and (c) as a general fallback the common law right to privacy. For an overview, see Solove, *The Digital Person*, 67–72, and for a compilation of these see Schwartz and Solove, *Information Privacy–Stat-utes and Regulations*. This complex patchwork of information privacy rights must leave citizens puzzled and confused as to what rights they enjoy, and under what conditions.

11. The conception gained prominence as the core principle of information privacy, as defined by Germany's Federal Constitutional Court in a case about the federal census (see BVerfGE 65, 1).

12. For the European Union, see Directive 95/46/EC on the protection of individuals with regard to the processing of personal data and on the free

movement of such data (European Union Data Protection Directive), OJ L 281, 23.11.1995, 31.

13. The term itself apparently was first used in the Steinmüller report to the German Parliament in the early 1970s.

14. See Olson, *The Logic of Collective Action*.

15. See, for example, Article 23 European Union Data Protection Directive "1. Member States shall provide that any person who has suffered damage as a result of an unlawful processing operation or of any act incompatible with the national provisions adopted pursuant to this Directive is entitled to receive compensation from the controller for the damage suffered. 2. The controller may be exempted from this liability, in whole or in part, if he proves that he is not responsible for the event giving rise to the damage." See also Section 7 and 8 of the German Federal Data Protection Act (Gesetz zum Schutz vor Mißbrauch personenbezogener Daten bei der Datenverarbeitung, BGBl.I 1990 S.2954), mandating no fault compensation and compensation for immaterial harm if the information processor is a government agency and a shift of the burden of proof for the private sector processors. See also, for example, Section 32 (permitting injunctions, giving the Data Protection Commission a role supporting individual complainants in liability proceedings) Austrian Federal Act Concerning the Protection of Personal Data (Datenschutzgesetz 2000, BGBl. I Nr. 165/1999).

16. This case and the data is taken from the excellent exposition in Seltzer and Anderson, "The Dark Side of Numbers."

17. Samuelson, "Privacy and Intellectual Property?"

18. Nissenbaum, "Privacy as Contextual Integrity."

19. Solove, *The Future of Reputation*.

20. Schwartz, "Property, Privacy, and Personal Data."

21. Laudon, "Markets and Privacy."

22. Lessig, *Code*, 160–62.

23. Digital Millennium Copyright Act § 103, 17 U.S.C.A. § 1201.

24. See Schwartz, "Beyond Lessig's Code for Internet Privacy"; Samuelson, "Privacy as Intellectual Property?"; Rotenberg, "Fair Information Practices and the Architecture of Privacy," ¶¶ 80–90; see also Lemley, "Private Property," 1547; Cohen, "DRM and Privacy," 577.

25. Mayer-Schönberger, "Beyond Copyright: Managing Information Rights with DRM."

26. Halderman, Waters, and Felten, "Privacy Management for Portable Recording Devices."

27. Julian Togelius, comment on Slashdot, May 10, 2007, http://yro.slashdot .org/comments.pl?sid=234167&cid=19065957.

28. Winter, "The Advantages of Amnesia."

29. Schacter, *How the Mind Forgets*, 184–206.
30. Anderson and Schooler, "Reflections of the Environment in Memory."
31. On the very extreme end of measures, drugs may be used to help such a cognitive adjustment. See in a different context, Kolber, "Therapeutic Forgetting: The Legal and Ethical Implications."
32. For a compelling description, see Heymann, *Terrorism, Freedom, and Security*.
33. Regarding second chances for individuals through the societal equivalent to expungement (e.g., in Victorian times), see Friedman, *Guarding Life's Dark Secrets*.
34. For an overview of expungement, see Michael D. Mayfield, "Revisiting Expungement: Concealing Information in the Information Age." For a call for federal expungement rules, see Fruqan Mouzon, "Forgive Us Our Trespasses: The Need for Federal Expungement Legislation." For a recent controversy about whether criminal records must be deleted or not, see Information Tribunal, The Chief Constable of Humberside and The Chief Constable of Staffordshire Police and The Chief Constable of Northumbria Police and The Chief Constable of West Midlands Police and The Chief Constable of Greater Manchester Police v. Information Commissioner, July 22, 2008, http://www.informationtribunal.gov.uk/DBFiles/Decision/i200/Chief_Constables_v_IC_final_decision_2007081_web_entry[1].pdf; see also, *BBC News*, "Criminal records 'must be erased.'"
35. See Lazer and Mayer-Schönberger, "Statutory Frameworks for Regulating Information Flows." Unfortunately, such deletion of DNA information may no longer be sufficient to remove an individual's genetic information from the criminal justice system. Recent advances in DNA search technology make it possible to identify individuals based on DNA information of relatives in the database, with deeply troubling implications for information privacy. See Bieber, Frederick R., Charles H. Brenner, and David Lazer, "Finding Criminals Through DNA of Their Relatives."
36. European Court of Human Rights, Grand Chamber Judgment, S. and Marper v. United Kingdom, December 4, 2008; see also *BBC News*, "DNA database 'breach of rights.'"
37. Directive 95/46/EC of the European Parliament and of the Council of 24 October 1995 on the protection of individuals with regard to the processing of personal data and on the free movement of such data, OJ 23 November 1995, No L. 281, 31.
38. Microsoft Privacy Guidelines for Developing Software Products and Services, Version 2.2, May 11, 2007, 11. While I serve on Microsoft's Trustworthy Computing Academic Advisory Board, I have had no role in drafting or otherwise shaping these guidelines nor have I ever been an employee of Microsoft.

39. Balkin, "The Constitution in the National Surveillance State," 21.
40. David Lazer and I have suggested this metaphor in Lazer and Mayer-Schönberger, "Statutory Frameworks for Regulating Information Flows."
41. See, for example, the International Money Laundering Abatement and Financial Anti-Terrorism Act of 2001 (also known as the U.S. Patriot Act Title III), Public Law No. 107–56, especially section 365 (anyone in business who transfers in excess of USD 10,000 in foreign currency has to file a report with Financial Crimes Enforcement Network - FinCEN).
42. In 2004, the U.S. Department of Homeland Security (DHS) required European commercial airlines to provide DHS with thirty-four information points for each passenger traveling to the U.S. by airplane before the aircraft had reached U.S. airspace. An agreement between DHS and the European Union was subsequently invalidated by the European Court of Justice. By 2007, DHS and the European Union had concluded a slightly less invasive arrangement that required the transfer of nineteen information fields per passenger (including name, all available contact information, payment information, travel itinerary, name of the travel agency that booked the flight, and baggage information). See Agreement between the European Union and the United States of America on the processing and transfer of Passenger Name Record (PNR) data by air carriers to the United States Department of Homeland Security (DHS) (2007 PNR Agreement), OJL 204, 4.8.2007, 18 (available at http://eur-lex.europa.eu/LexUriServ/LexUriServ.do?uri=OJ:L:2007:204:0018:0025:EN:PDF); see also the Electronic Privacy Information Center's excellent air travel privacy page at http://epic.org/privacy/airtravel/. On Senator Ted Kennedy finding himself on the U.S. federal no-fly list, see Sara Kehaulani Goo, "Sen. Kennedy Flagged by No-Fly List."
43. For the European Union, see Directive 2006/24/EC of the European Parliament and of the Council of 15 March 2006 on the retention of data generated or processed in connection with the provision of publicly available electronic communications services or of public communications networks and amending Directive 2002/58/EC, OJL 105, 13.04.2006, 54.
44. See especially Title IV of the Sarbanes-Oxley Act (also called the Public Company Accounting Reform and Investor Protection Act of 2002, Public Law No. 107–204, 116 Stat. 745) mandating additional disclosure of financial information.
45. The original Freedom of Information Act dates back to 1966 and the Johnson administration, but the statutes' current core was passed as amendments in 1974 and 1976 (Government in the Sunshine Act) as a direct reaction to the Watergate scandal.
46. See the 1990 Nutrition Labeling and Education Act (NLEA), Public Law No. 101–535.

47. See Directive 2003/4/EC of the European Parliament and of the Council of 28 January 2003 on public access to environmental information and repealing Council Directive 90/313/EEC, OJ L 41, 14.2.2003, 26.
48. In this context, it can be traced all the way back to Article 10 of the Council Directive 89/391/EEC of 12 June 1989 on the introduction of measures to encourage improvements in the safety and health of workers at work, OJ L 183, 29.6.1989, 1.
49. §§ 44a and 44b Abgeordnetengesetz and Verhaltensregeln für Mitglieder des Deutschen Bundestages.
50. See, for example, Lord, *The Perils and Promise of Global Transparency*. For a nuanced and cautious look at transparency, see Fung, Graham, and Weil, *Full Disclosure: The Perils and Promise of Transparency*.
51. Cheney and Dumcius, "Privacy Bill Stirs Concern Among Advertisers."
52. Brin, *The Transparent Society*, 331–33.
53. Gandy, *The Panoptic Sort*.
54. Brin, *The Transparent Society*, 333.
55. Gaudin, *Total Recall*.

Chapter 6. Reintroducing Forgetting

1. Mayer-Schönberger, "The Internet and Privacy Legislation: Cookies for a Treat?" *West Virginia Journal of Law & Technology* 1(1997): 1. An updated version was published as Mayer-Schönberger, "Internet Privacy: The Internet and Privacy Legislation: Cookies for a Treat?"
2. There is, of course, a subtle difference between "deleting" a file and actually physically erasing the information stored in it. When we "delete" a file, the bits containing its information are merely marked so they will be reused (and thus overwritten) when we store new information, but "deleting" a file does not physically reset the information bits. The more the information we store changes (for example because we add new information), the less dramatic the difference is. I am cognizant of the difference, and its consequences, but for the sake of readability I will continue to use "delete" in the untechnical sense.
3. See, for example, in the European Union the Council Directive 90/270/EEC of 29 May 1990 on the minimum safety and health requirements for work with display screen equipment (fifth individual Directive within the meaning of Article 16 (1) of Directive 89/391/EEC), OJL 156, 21.6.1990, 14, especially Annex, Section 3.
4. In fact, expiration dates may actually reduce expenses for information processors since less time and effort must be spent by them in separating the information wheat from the information chaff.
5. As cited in Rosen, "Google's Gatekeepers."

6. Such individual switching costs are different from the cost it takes to build a search engine (including a comprehensive search index). How high switching costs actually are is a hotly debated issue; contrast, for example, Telang, Mukhopadhyay, and Wilcox, "An Empirical Analysis of Internet Search Engine Choice," with Frank Pasquale and Oren Bracha, "Federal Search Commission?: Access, Fairness, and Accountability in the Law of Search."

7. Helft, "Google Adds a Safeguard on Privacy for Searchers."

8. American Civil Liberties Union v. Gonzales, No. 98–5591 (E.D. Pa.), available online at http://www.google.com/press/images/subpoena_20060317 .pdf.

9. Alberto Gonzales v. Google, Inc., No. CV 06–8006MISC JW (N.D. Ca.), available online at http://i.n.com.com/pdf/ne/2006/google_case.pdf.

10. Singel, "Google to Anonymize Data"; see also Rosen, "Google's Gatekeepers." To avoid being played out against each other by governments, major search engine providers recently crafted the Global Network Initiative that defines how they interact with governments around the world. See http://www.globalnetworkinitiative.org/.

11. "Microsoft and Ask.com Call on Industry to Join Together to Evolve Privacy Protections for Consumers," Microsoft Press Release, July 22, 2007.

12. Stone, "The Most Privacy-Friendly Search Engine on the Web Is . . . "

13. See Cuil at http://www.cuil.com/info/privacy/.

14. Helft, "Google Tightens Data Retention Policy–Again." Google's motives are not entirely clear. *The New York Times* article, as well as a report in the respected technoblog *Ars Technica* (Timmer, "Google Bows to EU Pressure, Cuts Data Retention Period Again") suggest it was mainly regulatory pressure from the European Union rather than competitive considerations that prompted Google to act. In their argument, they rely on an April 2008 opinion from the EU Working Party on Information Privacy (the so-called Article 29 Working Party). This is not entirely convincing, however, for two reasons. First, the EU report suggests that any retention date beyond six months would be considered "baseless" and in contradiction to EU law (Article 29 Data Protection Working Party, Opinion on data protection issues related to search engines, April 4, 2008, p. 25, available at http://ec.europa.eu/justice_home/fsj/privacy/index_en.htm). This is significantly shorter than the nine months Google settled on. Second, EU laws would only apply to information processing in the European Union, but Google announced a new retention policy for users the world over, most of which do not live in the European Union.

15. Microsoft Privacy Guidelines for Developing Software Products and Services, Version 2.2, May 11, 2007.

16. Council of the European Union, Transport, Telecommunications and Energy, Press Release, November 27, 2008, EN 16326/08 (Presse 345), 21.

17. Public Law No. 105–304.

18. Halderman, Waters, and Felten, "Privacy Management for Portable Recording Devices."

19. See, for example, Burger, "Vorbei, vergangen, vergessen?"

20. In fact, through the difference of logically deleting a file and physically erasing the information in it, already most of the file systems we use have a certain "decay" function built in: When we delete a file it is lost, but with a lot of effort some of the information can be recovered. How much depends on a number of factors, including how long after the initial deletion one attempts to recover information, and how much effort (and thus cost) one wants to expend.

21. For more information on the campaign, see *Apuntes e ideas sueltas* at http://www.apunteseideas.com/?p=404.

CHAPTER 7. CONCLUSIONS

1. See *HR Online*, "CDU feuert Vize der Jungen Union."

Bibliography

Agre, Phil and Marc Rotenberg, eds. *Technology and Privacy: The New Landscape*. Cambridge, MA: MIT Press. 1997.

Aimone, James B., Janet Wiles, and Fred H. Gage. "Computational Influence of Adult Neurogenesis on Memory Encoding." *Neuron* 61 (2009): 187–202.

Akerlof, George A. "The Market for 'Lemons': Quality Uncertainty and the Market Mechanism." *Quarterly Journal of Economics* 84 (1970): 488–500.

Anderson, Benedict. *Imagined Communities*. rev. ed. London: Verso. 1991.

Anderson, J. R. and L. J. Schooler. "Reflections of the Environment in Memory." *Psychological Science* 2 (1991): 396–408.

Arnsdorf, Isaac. "Seattle Attorney Finds that the Internet Won't Let Go of His Past." *The Seattle Times* (Aug. 17, 2008).

Associated Press. "Naked Photos, E-mail Get Teens in Trouble." *Fox News.com*. June 4, 2008. http://www.foxnews.com/story/0,2933,363438,00.html.

Atkinson, Robert D., Daniel K. Correa, and Julie A. Hedlund. "Explaining International Broadband Leadership." *The Information Technology and Innovation Foundation*. http://www.itif.org/index.php?id=142.

Baddeley, Alan. *Human Memory: Theory and Practice*. rev. ed. Hove: Psychology Press. 2003.

Bacon, Francis. *Essaies: religious meditations : places of perswasion and disswasion : seene and allowed*. London: John Laggard. 1606.

Baker, John C. et al. *Mapping the Risks: Assessing the Homeland Security Implications of Publicly Available Geospatial Information*. Santa Monica, CA: RAND. 2004.

Bakos, Yannis and Erik Brynjolfsson. "Bundling Information Goods: Pricing, Profits and Efficiency." *Management Science* 45 (Dec. 1999): 1613–30.

Balkin, Jack M. "The Constitution in the National Surveillance State." *Minnesota Law Review* 93 (2008): 1–25.

Bannon, Liam J. "Forgetting as a Feature, Not a Bug: The Duality of Memory and Implications for Ubiquitous Computing." *CoDesign* 2 (2006): 3–15.

Bayard, Pierre. *How to Talk About Books You Haven't Read.* New York: Bloomsbury. 2007.

BBC News. "Dishing the Dirt." Oct. 2, 2006. http://news.bbc.co.uk/2/hi/uk_news/magazine/5393088.stm.

———. "CCTV Boom 'Failing to Cut Crime.'" May 6, 2007. http://news.bbc.co.uk/go/pr/fr/-/2/hi/uk_news/7384843.stm.

———. "Identity 'at Risk' on Facebook." May 1, 2008. http://newsvote.bbc.co.uk/mpapps/pagetools/print/news.bbc.co.uk/2/hi/programmes/click_online/7375772.stm.

———. "Criminal Records 'Must Be Erased.'" July 22, 2008. http://news.bbc.co.uk/2/hi/uk_news/7520139.stm.

———. "DNA Database 'Breach of Rights.'" Dec. 4, 2008. http://news.bbc.co.uk/2/hi/uk_news/7764069.stm.

Bellia, Patricia. "The Memory Gap in Surveillance Law." *University of Chicago Law Review* 75 (2008): 137–79.

Benkler, Yochai. *The Wealth of Networks: How Social Production Transforms Markets and Freedom.* New Haven, CT: Yale University Press. 2006.

Bennett, Colin J. *Regulating Privacy. Data Protection and Public Policy in Europe and the United States.* Ithaca, NY: Cornell University Press. 1992.

Bentham, Jeremy. "Panopticon (Preface)," in *The Panopticon Writings,* Miran Bozovic, ed. 29–95. London: Verso. 1995.

Berg, Tom. "Remembering Every Day of Your Life." *The Orange County Register* (April 25, 2008): Life Section.

Berman, Francine. "Got Data? A Guide to Data Preservation in the Information Age." *Communications of the ACM* 51 (Dec. 2008): 50–56.

Bhatti, Jay and Jaideep Singh. *Spock.* http://www.spock.com/do/pages/pr_web_expo.

Bieber, Frederick R., Charles H. Brenner, and David Lazer. "Finding Criminals Through DNA of Their Relatives." *Science* 312.5778 (June 2, 2006): 1315–16.

Blackman, Josh. "Omniveillance, Google, Privacy in Public, and the Right to Your Digital Identity: A Tort for Recording and Disseminating an Individual's Image over the Internet." *Santa Clara Law Review* 49 (2008): 313–92.

Blanchette, Jean-François and Deborah G. Johnson. "Data Retention and the Panoptic Society: The Social Benefits of Forgetfulness." *The Information Society* 18 (2002): 33–45.

Borges, Jorge Luis. "Funes, His Memory" in *Collected Fictions*. Translated by Andrew Hurley. New York: Penguin. 1998.

Bredenkamp, Jürgen. *Lernen, Erinnern, Verstehen*. München: Beck. 1998.

Brin, David. *The Transparent Society*. Reading, MA: Addison-Wesley. 1998.

Brown, John Seely and Paul Duguid. *The Social Life of Information*. Cambridge, MA: Harvard Business School Press. 2002.

Burger, Reiner. "Vorbei, vergangen, vergessen?" *Frankfurter Allgemeine Sonntagszeitung* (Dec. 21, 2008): 10.

Burkert, Herbert. "Freedom of Information and Electronic Government," in *Governance and Information Technology—From Electronic Government to Information Government*, Viktor Mayer-Schönberger and David Lazer, eds. 125–41. Cambridge, MA: MIT Press. 2007.

Burt, Ronald. *Brokerage and Closure: An Introduction to Social Capital*. Oxford: Oxford University Press. 2005.

Bush, Vannevar. "A Vision of Hypertext," in *Visions of Technology*, Richard Rhodes, ed., 171–72. New York; Simon & Schuster. 1999.

BusinessWeek. "They Know What's in Your Medicine Cabinet." July 23, 2008. http://www.businessweek.com/magazine/content/08_31/ b4094000643943.htm?campaign_id=rss_daily.

Cabral, Luis M. B. and Ali Hortacsu. "The Dynamics of Seller Reputation: Theory and Evidence from eBay." CEPR Discussion Paper, No. 4345, April 2004. http://ssrn.com/abstract=541161.

Carruthers, Mary J. *The Book of Memory: A Study of Memory in Medieval Culture*. Cambridge: Cambridge University Press. 1990.

Casson, Lionel. *Libraries in the Ancient World*. New Haven, CT: Yale Nota Bene. 2001.

Castells, Manuel. *The Rise of the Network Society*. Oxford: Blackwell. 1996.

Cate, Fred. *Privacy in the Information Age*. Washington, DC: Brookings. 1997.

Cheney, Kyle and Gintautas Dumcius. "Privacy Bill Stirs Concern Among Advertisers." *Wakefield Observer* (July 8, 2008). http://www .wickedlocal.com/wakefield/homepage/x918303133/Privacy-bill-stirs-concern-among-advertisers.

Cohen, I. Bernard and Gregory W. Welch, eds. *Makin' Numbers: Howard Aiken and the Computer*. Cambridge, MA: MIT Press. 1999.

Cohen, Julie E. "DRM and Privacy." *Berkeley Technology Law Journal* 18 (2003): 575–617.

Cole, Simon A. *Suspect Identities: A History of Fingerprinting and Criminal Identification*. Cambridge, MA: Harvard University Press. 2002.

comScore Media Advisory. "Baidu Ranked Third Largest Worldwide Search Property by comScore in December 2007." News release. Jan. 24, 2008. http://www.comscore.com/press/release.asp?press=2018.

Curry, Michael R. "Location and Identity: A Brief History," in *RFID: Applications, Security, and Privacy*, S. L. Garfinkel and B. Rosenberg, eds. 149–62. Saddle River, NJ: Addison-Wesley. 2005.

———. "Toward a Geography of a World without Maps: Lessons from Ptolemy and Postal Codes." *Annals of the Association of American Geographers* 95 (2005): 680–91.

Deering, Michael F. *The Limits of Human Vision*. http://www.swift.ac.uk/vision.pdf.

Dellarocas, Chrysanthos. "Analyzing the Economic Efficiency of eBay-like Online Reputation Reporting Mechanisms," MIT Sloan Working Paper No. 4181–01, Oct. 2001. http://ssrn.com/abstract=289968 or DOI: 10.2139/ssrn.289968.

Diffie, Whitfield and Susan Landau. *Privacy on the Line: The Politics of Wiretapping and Encryption*. Cambridge, MA: MIT Press. 2007.

Dillenz, Walter. "Druckprivilegien und Drucker zwischen Kapitalismus und europäischem Religionsstreit," in *Die Notwendigkeit des Urheberrechtsschutzes im Lichte seiner Geschichte*, Robert Dittrich, ed. 46–49. Wien, Austria: Manz. 1991.

Doctorow, Cory. *Scroogled*. http://blogoscoped.com/archive/207-09-17-n72.html. Sept. 17, 2007.

Drogin, Marc. *Anathema! Medieval Scribes and the History of Book Curses*. Totowa, N.J.: Allanheld, Osmun. 1983.

The Economist. "The Hidden Revolution: Special Report on Telecoms." April 28, 2007.

———. "H.M." Dec. 18, 2008. 146.

———. "Everybody Does It: Who Has a Closet without a Skeleton?" Jan. 2, 2009.

Eco, Umberto. *Lector in Fabula: La cooperazione interpretativa nei test narrativi*. Milan: Studi Bompiani. 1979.

Edwards, Mark U. *Printing, Propaganda, and Martin Luther*. Berkeley, CA: University of California Press. 1994.

Eisenstein, Elizabeth L. *The Printing Revolution in Early Modern Europe*. Cambridge: Canto/Cambridge University Press. 1993.

Eliot, Simon. "Never Mind the Value, What about the Price? Or, How Much Did *Marmion* Cost St. John Rivers?," *Nineteenth-Century Literature* 56 (2001): 160–97.

Eliot, T. S. *Burnt Norton*. London: Faber & Faber. 1941.

Fay, Patrick J. "Worldwide Fiber and Cable: Demand, Production, and Price." *Lightwave*. (undated). http://lw.pennnet.com/articles/article _display.cfm?article_id=35508.

Febvre, Lucien and Henri-Jean Martin. *The Coming of the Book*. London: Verso. 2000.

Fish, Stanley. *Is There a Text in This Class? The Authority of Interpretive Communities*. Cambridge, MA: Harvard University Press. 1982.

Flaherty, David H. *Protecting Privacy in Surveillance Societies. The Federal Republic of Germany, Sweden, France, Canada, and the United States*. Chapel Hill, NC: The University of North Carolina Press. 1989.

Foer, Joshua. "Remember This." *National Geographic* (Nov. 2007): 32–55.

Foucault, Michel. *Discipline and Punish: The Birth of the Prison*. New York: Random House. 1975.

Friedman, Lawrence M. *Guarding Life's Dark Secrets: Legal and Social Controls over Reputation, Propriety, and Privacy*. Stanford: Stanford University Press. 2007.

Fung, Archon, Mary Graham, and David Weil. *Full Disclosure: The Perils and Promise of Transparency*. Cambridge: Cambridge University Press. 2007.

Gandy, Oscar H. *The Panoptic Sort: A Political Economy of Personal Information*. Boulder, CO: Westview. 1993.

Garfinkel, Simson. *Database Nation: The Death of Privacy in the 21st Century*. Sebastopol, CA: O'Reilly. 2000.

Gaudin, Sharon. "Total Recall: Storing Every Life Memory in a Surrogate Brain." *Computerworld* (April 2, 2008).

Gillette, Clayton. "Reputation and Intermediaries in Electronic Commerce." *Louisiana Law Review* 62 (2002): 1165–97.

Glendinning, Chellis. *My Name is Chellis and I'm in Recovery from Western Civilization*. Gabriola Island, BC: New Catalyst Books. 2007.

Goo, Sara Kehaulani. "Sen. Kennedy Flagged by No-Fly List." *The Washington Post* (Aug. 20, 2004): A01.

Gorman, Siobhan, "NSA's Domestic Spying Grows as Agency Sweeps up Data." *The Wall Street Journal* (March 10, 2008): A1.

Graff, Harvey J. *The Legacies of Literacy*. Bloomington, IN: Indiana University Press. 1991.

Graham, Mary. *Democracy by Disclosure: The Rise of Technopopulism*. Washington, DC: Brookings. 2002.

Greenwald, Glenn. "What Does Sarah Palin Have to Hide in Her Yahoo E-mails?" *Salon.com*. Sept. 18, 2008. http://www.salon.com/ opinion/greenwald/2008/09/18/privacy/.

Griswold, Charles L. *Forgiveness: A Philosophical Exploration*. New York: Cambridge University Press. 2007.

Habermas, Jürgen. *The Structural Transformation of the Public Sphere: An Inquiry into a Category of Bourgeois Society*. Cambridge: MIT Press, 1991.

Halderman, J. Alex, Brent R. Waters, and Edward W. Felten. "Privacy Management for Portable Recording Devices." Workshop on Privacy in Electronic Society, November 2004.

Hansell, Saul. "Sellers Give Negative Feedback on eBay Changes." *The New York Times* (Jan. 29, 2008). http://bits.blogs.nytimes.com/2008/01/29/sellers-give-negative-feedback-on-ebay-changes/?ref=technology.

HarrisInteractive, *The Harris Poll #40*. http://www.harrisinteractive.com.

Harris, Robert. *Selling Hitler*. New York: Pantheon, 1986.

Hasbrouck, Edward. "What's in a Passenger Name Record (PNR)?" *The Practical Nomad*. http://hasbrouck.org/articles/PNR.html.

Helft, Miguel. "Google Adds a Safeguard on Privacy for Searchers." *The New York Times* (March 15, 2007). http://www.nytimes.com/2007/03/15/technology/15googles.html?_r=1&oref=slogin.

———. "Google Tightens Data Retention Policy: Again." *The New York Times* (Sept. 9, 2008). http://bits.blogs.nytimes.com/2008/09/09/google-tightens-data-retention-policy-again/?ref=technology.

Heymann, Philip B. *Terrorism, Freedom, and Security: Winning Without War*. Cambridge, MA: MIT Press. 2003.

Houser, Daniel and John C. Wooders. "Reputation in Auctions: Theory, and Evidence from eBay." *Journal of Economics & Management Strategy* 15 (2006): 353–69.

Howard, Bill. "Analyzing Online Social Networks." *Communications of the ACM* 51 (Nov. 2008): 14–16.

HR Online. "CDU feuert Vize der Jungen Union." May 22, 2008. http://www.hr-online.de/website/rubriken/nachrichten/index.jsp?rubrik=5710&key=standard_document_34336030.

Jones, Steven E. *Against Technology: From Luddites to Neo-Luddism*. New York: Routledge. 2006.

Keohane, Robert O. and Joseph S. Nye, Jr. "Power and Interdependence in the Information Age." *Foreign Affairs* 77 (1998): 81–94.

Kilgour, Frederick G. *The Evolution of the Book*. New York: Oxford University Press. 1998.

King, David. *The Commissar Vanishes: The Falsification of Photographs and Art in Stalin's Russia*. New York: Metropolitan Books. 1997.

Kolber, Adam. "Therapeutic Forgetting: The Legal and Ethical Implications of Memory Dampening." *Vanderbilt Law Review* 59 (2006): 1561–626.

Kopelev, Lev. *To Be Preserved Forever*. Philadelphia: Lippincott. 1977.

Krebs, Brian. "Teen Pleads Guilty to Hacking Paris Hilton's Phone." *The Washington Post* (Sept. 13, 2005).

Kreimer, Seth F. "Watching the Watchers: Surveillance, Transparency, and Political Freedom in the War on Terror." *University of Pennsylvania Journal of Constitutional Law* 7 (2004): 133–82.

Lasica, J. D. "The Net Never Forgets." *Salon.com* (Nov. 25, 1998). http://archive.salon.com/21st/feature/1998/11/25feature2.html.

Laudon, Kenneth C. "Markets and Privacy." *Communications of the ACM* (Sept. 1996): 92–104.

Lazer, David and Viktor Mayer-Schönberger. "Statutory Frameworks for Regulating Information Flows: Drawing Lessons for the DNA Data Banks from Other Government Data Systems." *Journal of Law, Medicine & Ethics* 34 (2006): 366–74.

Lee, B. *The Social and Class Structure of Early Chosun: Korean History*. Vol. 23. Seoul, Korea: National History Publication Committee. 1994.

Lee, Ronald and Paul Schwartz. "Heymann: Terrorism, Freedom and Security." *Michigan Law Review* 103 (2005): 1446–82.

Leggat, Robert. *A History of Photography from Its Beginnings till the 1920s*. http://www.rleggat.com/photohistory/index.html.

Lemley, Mark A. "Private Property." *Stanford Law Review* 52 (2000): 1545–57.

Lenhart, Amanda, Mary Madden, Alexandra Rankin Macgill, and Aaron Smith. "Teen Content Creators." *Pew Internet & American Life Project* (Dec. 19, 2007). http://pewresearch.org/pubs/670/teen-content-creators.

Lessig, Lawrence. *Code: And Other Laws of Cyberspace*. New York: Basic Books. 1999.

———. *Change Congress*. http://change-congress.org.

Levy, Andrew. "Teenage Office Worker Sacked for Moaning on Facebook about Her 'Totally Boring' Job." *The Daily Mail*, Feb. 26, 2009. http://www.dailymail.co.uk/news/article-1155971/Teenage-office-worker-sacked-moaning-Facebook-totally-boring-job.html.

Liptak, Adam. "The Nation's Borders, Now Guarded by the Net." *The New York Times* (May 14, 2007). http://select.nytimes.com/2007/05/14/us/14bar.html?_r=1&scp=1&sq=The%20Nation%E2%80%99s%20Borders,%20Now%20Guarded%20by%20the%20Net&st=cse.

Loke, Margarett. "Photography Review; In a John Brown Portrait, The Essence of a Militant." *The New York Times* (July 7, 2000): Arts.

Lord, Kristin M. *The Perils and Promise of Global Transparency*. Albany, NY: SUNY Press. 2006.

Lyman, Peter and Hal R. Varian. *How Much Information?* http://www.sims
.berkeley.edu/how-much-info-2003.

Man, John. *The Gutenberg Revolution: The Story of a Genius that Changed the
World.* London: Review. 2002.

MAPlight.org Money and Politics: Illuminating the Connection. http://www
.maplight.org.

Markoff, John. "H.P. Reports Big Advance in Memory Chip Design." *The
New York Times* (May 1, 2008). http://www.nytimes.com/2007/
09/11/technology/11storage.html?ex=1347163200&en=
26735eaee1d37b46&ei=5088&partner=rssnyt&emc=rss.

Maron, Monika. *Flugasche.* Frankfurt am Main: Fischer. 1981.

Martin, Henri-Jean. *Print, Power, and People in 17th-Century France.*
Metuchen, NJ: Scarecrow Press. 1993.

Mayer-Schönberger, Viktor. "Generational Development of Data Protection
in Europe," in *Technology and Privacy: The New Landscape*, Phil
Agre and Marc Rotenberg, eds. 219–41. Cambridge, MA: MIT
Press. 1997.

———. "Internet Privacy: The Internet and Privacy Legislation: Cookies for a
Treat?" *Computer Law & Securities Report* 14 (1998): 166–74.

———. *Information und Recht: Vom Datenschutz bis zum Urheberrecht.*
Vienna, Austria: Springer. 2001.

———. "Beyond Copyright: Managing Information Rights with DRM." *Denver University Law Review* 84 (2006): 181–98.

Mayer-Schönberger, Viktor and David Lazer. "From Electronic Government
to Information Government," in *Governance and Information Technology: From Electronic Government to Information Government,*
Viktor Mayer-Schönberger and David Lazer, eds. 1–14. Cambridge, MA: MIT Press. 2007.

Mayer-Schönberger, Viktor and Gernot Brodnig. "Information Power: International Affairs in the Cyber Age." Kennedy School Working Paper
Number RWP01–044 (2001).

Mayfield, Michael D. "Revisiting Expungement: Concealing Information in
the Information Age." *Utah Law Review* 1997: 1057–85.

McNeill, J. R. and William H. McNeill. *The Human Web. A Bird's-Eye View of
World History.* New York: Norton. 2003.

Microsoft, "Privacy Principles for Live Search and Online Ad Targeting."
July 23, 2007. http://download.microsoft.com/download/3/7/
f/37f14671-ddee-499b-a794-077b3673f186/Microsoft%E2%80%
99s%20Privacy%20Principles%20for%20Live%20Search%20and%
20Online%20Ad%20Targeting.pdf.

Miller, Arthur R. *The Assault on Privacy: Computers, Data Banks and Dossiers.* Ann Arbor: University of Michigan Press. 1971.

Minkel, J. R. "Hard Disk Recovered from Columbia Shuttle Solves Physics Problem." *Scientific American* (May 5, 2008). http://www.sciam.com/article.cfm?id=hard-disk-recovered-from-columbia&print=true.

Moore, Gordon E. "Progress in Digital Integrated Electronics," in *Visions of Technology*, Richard Rhodes, ed. 243. New York; Simon & Schuster. 1999.

Morris County Library. http://www.gti.net/mocolib1/prices/.

Mouzon, Fruqan. "Forgive Us Our Trespasses: The Need for Federal Expungement Legislation." *University of Memphis Law Review* 39 (2008): 1–46.

Mowery, David and Nathan Rosenberg. "The Influence of Market Demand Upon Innovation: A Critical Review of Some Recent Empirical Studies." Reprinted in Nathan Rosenberg, *Inside the Black Box: Technology and Economics*. 193–243. Cambridge: Cambridge University Press. 1982.

Mühe, Ulrich, Ulrich Tukur, Sebastian Koch, and Martina Gedeck. *The Lives of Others*. DVD. Directed by Florian Henckel von Donnersmarck. Culver City, CA: Sony Pictures Classics. 2006.

Musil, Steven. "Facebook Hits 175 Million User Mark." *CNET* (Feb. 15, 2009). http://news.cnet.com/8301-1023_3-10164458-93.html?part=rss&subj=news&tag=2547-1_3-0-20.

Negroponte, Nicholas. *Being Digital*. New York: Alfred Knopf. 1995.

New Paradigm Resources Group. "Dark Fiber: Means to a Network." *Competitive Telecoms Issues* 10 (Feb. 2002): 1–14. http://www.fibertech.com/docs/MeansToANetwork.pdf.

Nissenbaum, Helen. "Privacy as Contextual Integrity." *Washington Law Review* 79 (2004): 119–57.

Nozick, Robert. *Philosophical Explanations*. Oxford: Clarendon Press. 1981.

Null, Christopher. "Drunken Pirate Says 'Be Careful What You Post Online.'" *Yahoo! Tech*. April 30, 2007. http://tech.yahoo.com/blogs/null/25755.

Oakley, William S. "E-Beam Hard Disk Drive Using Gated Carbon Nano Tube Source and Phase Change Media." 24th IEEE Conference on Mass Storage Systems and Technologies (MSST 2007): 245–50.

OECD Directorate for Science, Technology, and Industry. 2007. *Broadband Statistics to June 2007*. http://www.oecd.org/sti/ict/broadband.

Olson, Mancur. *The Logic of Collective Action*. Cambridge, MA: Harvard University Press. 1971.

OMB Watch. *EPA Email to Direct Connect Users*. http://www.ombwatch.org/article/articleview/213/1/1/#EPA.

Orwell, George. *1984*. New York: Penguin. 1983.

Palfrey, John and Urs Gasser. *Born Digital: Understanding the First Generation of Digital Natives*. New York: Basic Books. 2008.

Parker, Elizabeth S., Larry Cahill, and James L McGaugh. "A Case of Unusual Autobiographical Remembering." *Neurocase* 12 (2006): 35–49.

Pasquale, Frank and Oren Bracha. "Federal Search Commission?: Access, Fairness and Accountability in the Law of Search." University of Texas School Law Public Law and Legal Theory Research Paper No. 123. July 2007.

Pear, Robert. "In Digital Age, Federal Files Blip Into Oblivion." *The New York Times* (Sept. 13, 2008). http://www.nytimes.com/2008/09/13/us/13records.html?scp=1&sq=In%20Digital%20Age,%20Federal%20Files%20Blip%20Into%20Oblivion&st=cse.

Pinheiro, Eduoardo, Wolf-Dietrich Weber, and Luiz André Barroso. "Failure Trends in a Large Disk Drive Population." Google research paper. http://research.google.com/archive/disk_failures.pdf.

Price, Jill. *The Woman Who Can't Forget: The Extraordinary Story of Living with the Most Remarkable Memory Known to Science.* With Bart Davis. New York: Free Press. 2008.

Priedhorsky, Reid, Jilin Chen, Shyong (Tony) K. Lam, Katherine Panciera, Loren Terveen, and John Riedl. "Creating, Destroying, and Restoring Value in Wikipedia," in *Proceedings of the 2007 International ACM Conference on Supporting Group Work.* Sanibel Island, Florida, Nov. 4–7, 2007. New York: ACM. 259–68. DOI= http://doi.acm.org/10.1145/1316624.1316663.

Proust, Marcel. *In Search of Lost Time.* New York: Modern Library. 2003.

Resnick, Paul and Richard Zeckhauser. "Trust Among Strangers in Internet Transactions: Empirical Analysis of eBay's Reputation System," in *Advances in Applied Microeconomics*, Michael R. Baye, ed. *Volume 11*, 127–57. Amsterdam: Elsevier Science. 2002.

Roberts, Alasdair. *Blacked Out: Government Secrecy in the Information Age.* Cambridge: Cambridge University Press. 2006.

Rose, Mark. *Authors and Owners: The Invention of Copyright.* Cambridge, MA: Harvard University Press. 1993.

Rose-Redwood, Reuben S. "Indexing the Great Ledger of the Community: Urban House Numbering, City Directories, and the Production of Spatial Legibility." *Journal of Historical Geography* 34 (2008): 286–310.

Rosen, Jeffrey. *The Unwanted Gaze: The Destruction of Privacy in America.* New York: Random House. 2000.

———. *The Naked Crowd: Reclaiming Security and Freedom in an Anxious Age.* New York: Random House. 2004.

———. "Google's Gatekeepers." *The New York Times* (Nov. 30, 2008). http://www.nytimes.com/2008/11/30/magazine/30google-t.html?_r=1&scp=1&sq=Google%E2%80%99s%20Gatekeepers&st=cse.

Rossington, Michael and Anne Whitehead, eds. *Theories of Memory: A Reader*. Baltimore, MD: The Johns Hopkins University Press. 2007.

Rotenberg, Marc. "Fair Information Practices and the Architecture of Privacy: (What Larry Doesn't Get)." *Stanford Technology Law Review* (Feb. 2001). http://stlr.stanford.edu/.

Rubinstein, Ira S., Ronald D. Lee, and Paul M Schwartz. "Data Mining and Internet Profiling: Emerging Regulatory and Technological Approaches." *University of Chicago Law Review* 75 (2008): 261–85.

Rule, James B. *Privacy in Peril: How We Are Sacrificing a Fundamental Right in Exchange for Security and Convenience*. New York: Oxford University Press. 2007.

Samuelson, Pamela. "Privacy as Intellectual Property?" *Stanford Law Review* 52 (2000): 1125–73.

Schacter, Daniel L. *How the Mind Forgets and Remembers. The Seven Sins of Memory*. Boston: Houghton Mifflin. 2001.

Schaff, Philip. *History of the Christian Church*. Peabody, Massachusetts: Hendrickson Publishers. 2006.

Schmandt-Besserat, Denise. *How Writing Came About*. Austin, TX: University of Texas Press. 1992.

Schramm, William. "The Cost of Books in Chaucer's Time." *Modern Language* 3 (1933): 139–45.

Schroeder, Bianca and Garth A. Gibson. "Disk Failures in the Real World: What Does an MTTF of 1,000,000 Hours Mean to You." Paper presented at FAST '07: 5th USENIX Conference on File and Storage Technologies. 2007. http://www.cs.cmu.edu/~bianca/fast07.pdf.

Schulman, Daniel. "What Was gwb@whitehouse.gov Really Up To?" *Mother Jones* (Sept./Oct. 2008). http://www.motherjones.com/news/feature/2008/09/exit-strategy-control-delete-escape.html.

Schwartz, Paul M. "Beyond Lessig's Code for Internet Privacy: Cyberspace Filters, Privacy Control, and Fair Information Practices." *Wisconsin Law Review* (2000): 743–88.

———. "Property, Privacy, and Personal Data." *Harvard Law Review* 117 (2004): 2056–128.

Schwartz, Paul and Daniel J. Solove. *Information Privacy: Statutes and Regulations, 2008–2009*. New York: Aspen Publishers. 2008.

Seltzer, William and Margo Anderson. "The Dark Side of Numbers: The Role of Population Data Systems in Human Rights Abuses." *Social Research* 68 (2001): 481–513.

Shapiro, Carl and Hal R. Varian. *Information Rules: A Strategic Guide to the Network Economy*. Cambridge, MA: Harvard Business School Press. 1998.

Singtel, Ryan. "Google to Anonymize Data." *Wired Blog Network*. March 14, 2007. http://blog.wired.com/27bstroke6/2007/03/google_to_anony .html.

Slobogin, Christopher. *Privacy at Risk: The New Government Surveillance and the Fourth Amendment*. Chicago: University of Chicago Press. 2007.

Smith, Steven W. *The Scientist and Engineer's Guide to Digital Signal Processing*. San Diego, CA: California Technical Publishing. 1998.

Solove, Daniel J. *The Digital Person: Technology and Privacy in the Information Age*. New York City: New York University Press. 2004.

———. *The Future of Reputation*. New Haven: Yale University Press, 2007.

Solove, Daniel J., Marc Rotenberg, and Paul Schwartz. *Information Privacy Law*. New York: Aspen Publishers. 2006.

———. *Privacy, Information, and Technology*. New York: Aspen Publishers, 2006.

Spence, Michael. "Signaling in Retrospect and the Informational Structure of Markets." *American Economic Review* 92 (2002): 434–59.

Starbuck, William H. "Unlearning Ineffective or Obsolete Technologies." *International Journal of Technology Management* 11 (1996): 725–37.

Starr, Paul. *The Creation of the Media: Political Origins of Modern Communications*. New York: Basic Books. 2004.

Stiglitz, Joseph E. and Ann Florini. *The Right to Know: Transparency for an Open World*. New York: Columbia University Press. 2007.

Stone, Brad. "The Most Privacy-Friendly Search Engine on the Web Is . . . " *The New York Times* (July 23, 2007). http://bits.blogs.nytimes.com/ 2007/07/23/the-most-privacy-friendly-search-engine-on-the-web-is/.

Telang, Rahul, Tridas Mukhopadhyay, and Ronald Wilcox, "An Empirical Analysis of Internet Search Engine Choice." Darden School of Business Working Paper No. 03–05. 2003.

Telegeography. *Global Bandwidth Research Service*. Washington, DC: PriMetrica 2008. Executive Summary available free of charge at http://www.telegeography.com/products/gb/index.php.

Thompson, Clive. "A Head for Detail," in *The Best of Technology Writing*, Steven Levy, ed. 94–114. Ann Arbor, MI: The University of Michigan Press. 2007.

Timmer, John. "Google Bows to EU Pressure, Cuts Data Retention Period Again." *Ars Technica* (Sept. 9, 2008). http://arstechnica.com/news .ars/post/20080909-google-bows-to-eu-pressure-cuts-data-retention-period-agaom.html.

Vaidhyanathan, Siva. *The Anarchist in the Library: How the Clash Between Freedom and Control Is Hacking the Real World and Crashing the System*. New York City: Basic Books. 2004.

Van der Spiegel, Jan et al. "The ENIAC," in *The First Computers: History and Architectures*, Raúl Rojas and Ulf Hashagen, eds. 130–32. Cambridge, MA: MIT Press. 2000.

Wagenaar, Willem. "My Memory: A Study of Autobiographical Memory over Six Years." *Cognitive Psychology* 18 (1986): 225–52.

Walter, Chip. "Kryder's Law." *Scientific American* (July 2005). http://www.sciam.com/article.cfm?id=kryders-law.

Warren, Samuel and Louis Brandeis. "The Right to Privacy." *Harvard Law Review* 4 (1890): 193–220.

Watzlawick, P., J. H. Beavin, and D. D. Jackson. *Pragmatics of Human Communication: A Study of Interactional Patterns, Pathologies, and Paradoxes.* New York: W. W. Norton & Company. 1967.

Westin, Alan F. *Privacy and Freedom.* New York: Atheneum. 1967.

Whitaker, Reg. *The End of Privacy.* New York: The New Press. 1999.

Wilkinson, Alec. "Remember This?: A Project to Record Everything We Do in Life." *The New Yorker* (May 28, 2007).

Williamson, Samuel H. *Five Ways to Compute the Relative Value of a U.S. Dollar Amount, 1790 to Present.* http://measuringworth.com/.

Winter, Jessica. "The Advantages of Amnesia." *Boston Globe.* Sept. 23, 2007. http://www.boston.com/news/globe/ideas/articles/2007/09/23/the_advantages_of_amnesia/?page=full.

Wired. "Raw Data." April 2000. http://www.wired.com/wired/archive/8.04/mustread.html?pg=15.

Wixted, John T. and Shana K. Carpenter. "The Wickelgren Power Law and the Ebbinghaus Savings Function." *Psychological Science* 18 (2007): 133–34.

Yu, Peter K. "Of Monks, Medieval Scribes, and Middlemen." *Michigan State Law Review* 2006: 1–31.

Zachary, G. Pascal. *Endless Frontier. Vannevar Bush, Engineer of the American Century.* New York: Free Press. 1997.

Zick, Timothy. "Clouds, Cameras, and Computers: The First Amendment and Networked Public Places." *Florida Law Review* 59 (2007): 1–69.

Zittrain, Jonathan. *The Future of the Internet and How to Stop It.* New Haven: Yale University Press. 2008.

Index

82–83; property of, 143; quality of,
96–97; recall of, 18–19; recombining
of, 61–62, 85, 88–90; recontextualiza-
tion of, 89–90; retrieval of, 72–79; risk
of collecting, 158; role of, 85; self-
disclosure of, 4; sharing of, 3, 84–85;
total amount of, 52
information control: relational concepts
of, 153
information dossiers, 104; digital, 123–25
information ecology, 157–63
information power, 112; differences in,
107, 133, 187, 191, 192
information privacy, 100, 108, 135, 174,
181–82; effectiveness of rights to, 135–
36, 139–40, 143–44; enforcement of
right to, 139–40; purpose limitation
principle in, 136, 138, 159; rights to,
134–44
information retrieval. See information:
retrieval of
information sharing: default of, 88
information storage: capacity, 66; cheap,
62–72; corporate, 68–69; density of,
71; economics of, 68; increase in, 71–
72; magnetic, 62–64; optical, 64–65;
relative cost of, 65–66; sequential nature of analog, 75
informational self-determination, 137;
relational dimension of, 170
intellectual property (IP), 144, 146, 150,
174
Internet, 79; "future proof," 59–60; peer-
production and, 131–32
Internet archives, 4
Islam: printing in, 40
Ito, Joi, 126

Johnson, Deborah, 14

Keohane, Robert, 98
Kodak, Eastman, 45–46
Korea: printing in, 40

language, 23–28
Lasica, J. D., 14

Laudon, Kenneth, 145–46
law enforcement, 9
Lazer, David, 159
Lessig, Lawrence, 145–46
library, 33, 36, 74, 190; of Ashurbanipal,
33, 36; of Ptolemy, 33
literacy, 40, 41–42, 45
Luddites, 129
Luther, Martin, 38–39, 98

MAD megadisco, 5–6
markets, 10
mass media, 43–44
McNeill, J. R., 25
McNeill, William, 25
medical records, 9
memex, 51
memory, 125; accessibility of digital,
101–3; alterability of, 120–22, 126;
comprehensiveness of digital, 103–5,
122, 166; cost of analog, 45–49,
72–75; declarative, 19; digital, 118; di-
vergence of, 119; durability of digital,
103; episodic, 19, 25, 33; external,
28–49; human, 16–23; as living construct, 20; long-term, 18–21; misattri-
bution of, 20; to overcome human
mortality, 23, 91; procedural, 18–19,
24; reconstructing, 122; shared, 28,
42–45; short-term, 17–18; suggestibility of, 20; superior (hyperthymestic),
21; temporal dimension of shared, 43;
trust in, 119–22, 123, 126; value of,
126
Mesopotamia, 31
meta-information, 77, 79, 144–45, 149,
178, 179
metadata. See meta-information
Microsoft, 6, 8, 50, 51, 159, 176–78,
179
Miller, Arthur, 11, 100
misinterpretation: danger of, 90
Moore, Gordon, 63–64
Moore's law, 64
MyLifeBits, 50–51
MySpace, 1, 2, 84, 102, 131